C $\overline{\frac{OE}{121}}$

ADAPTATION IN LANGUAGE TEACHING

AUSGEM
Inst
für Anglistik, /
und Ke
Universi

D1729748

Harold S. Madsen

Brigham Young University

J. Donald Bowen

University of California at Los Angeles

Bibliothek
Englisches Seminar
Universität Bonn

/ NEWBURY HOUSE PUBLISHERS, INC. / ROWLEY / MASS /

820344

Library of Congress Cataloging in Publication Data

Madsen, Harold S
  Adaptation in language teaching.

  1. Language and languages--Study and teaching.
2. Text-books. 3. Lesson planning. I. Bowen,
Jean Donald, 1922-   joint author. II. Title.
P53.B65   407   78-783
ISBN 0-88377-105-5

Cover type design by Wendy Doherty.
Cover art by Barbara Frake.

NEWBURY HOUSE PUBLISHERS, INC.

Language Science
Language Teaching
Language Learning

ROWLEY, MASSACHUSETTS 01969

Copyright © 1978 by Newbury House Publishers, Inc. All rights reserved. No part
of this book may be reproduced or transmitted in any form or by any means, elec-
tronic or mechanical, including photocopying, recording, or by any information
storage and retrieval system, without permission in writing from the Publisher.

First printing: May 1978

Printed in the U.S.A.   5   4   3   2

TO
MONA and KAY
and our families

CONTENTS

FOREWORD

The traditional sources of recognition within the language teaching profession have been the writing of materials and the devising of methods for other teachers to use. But the success, either of methods or of materials, depends on what their users do with them. The lubricant for this crucial interstice consists of what Bowen and Madsen call "particularizing" and "adaptation." The latter, perhaps because it is undertaken for the benefit of relatively small and local groups of students, rather than for a wider audience of professional colleagues, has been less honored, and therefore less studied, than materials writing and methods have.

In the late 1960s, I became concerned about the need for more consistent attention to the art of adaptation, and went so far as to write a book about it (1971). That book, however, emerged primarily from the flood of materials produced between World War II and 1970 for the seldom-taught languages. Not only were the languages themselves unfamiliar to most readers; the settings in which the materials had been used—Peace Corps training programs, small university courses, etc.—were also quite different from the circumstances in which the vast majority of language teachers work.

The work of Bowen and Madsen, by contrast, is drawn from their considerable experience with the mainstream of foreign language teaching around the world. This fact alone gives to their work a high degree of credibility. Their many examples, moreover, are paraphrased from a wide range of actual textbooks in frequently taught languages. In effect, two master craftsmen are inviting the reader (or the trainee teacher) to walk at their side as they deal with a broad spectrum of the practical issues that we all face as we ply our trade. And because the examples are so very typical, they will serve as excellent starting points and models for numerous projects in the teacher training course. The book is therefore not only credible, but also eminently usable.

Finally, I am refreshed by the authors' emphasis on "congruence" (again, an interstitial concept), rather than on conformity to yet another set of standards or criteria.

Earl W. Stevick

Arlington, Virginia

June 1977

INTRODUCTION

Every teacher is in a very real sense an adapter of the textbook or materials he uses. No matter how logically organized and carefully written the text, the teacher will have his own ideas about the material to be presented and the manner of presentation. This would be true even if a teacher used the "ideal text": one he had written himself, on a subject he was fully competent in, for a group of students whose problems and abilities he knew intimately. The reason, of course, is that the good teacher is constantly adapting. He adapts when he adds an example not found in the book or when he telescopes an assignment by having students prepare "only the even-numbered items." He adapts even when he refers to an exercise covered earlier, or when he introduces a supplementary picture, song, realia, or report. While a conscientious author tries to anticipate questions that may be raised by his readers, the teacher can respond not merely to verbal questions (some of which the author could not anticipate), but even to the raised eyebrows of his students. This most useful guidance indicates when further explication, more examples, or greater detail is needed. But it would be a trivial exercise to write a special book to tell teachers that it is necessary to particularize teaching materials in a classroom; this is the heart of teaching and should be a prominent concern in any teacher-training course.

Often, however, textbooks need more than the usual "interpretation." It sometimes happens that in a class where oral communication is a prominent goal, the text may not provide sufficient oral activity. In another class the language book may not provide adequately challenging grammar practice for the more advanced students. Or a teacher with an audio-lingual orientation may find himself out of step with the presentation in his situational text. In brief, even when a text is well written, it may not be completely compatible with the instructional aims, student level, or teaching style in a given school or classroom.

And language textbooks are not without their flaws. For one thing, texts tend to date as they grow older, as theories and methods change and develop. Also, it is a rare book in which every set of exercises is appropriately idiomatic and reflective of real-life communication. Quite a number of books contain flaws in language presentation, obsolescent explanations, or even errors in the description of the structure of the language.

Adaptation is often required in order to increase motivation for learning—by making the language more real, the situations more relevant, the illustrations (visual or printed) more vivid and interesting. It is sometimes required to ensure greater ease of acquisition—by providing sufficient practice, logical explanations, plus examples or exercises that are on the level of the learner. It may be needed to ensure appropriate, accurate, and effective communicative competence—by developing an awareness of socially legitimate applications for given expressions or through exposure to bona fide contemporary usage.

Obviously, when very extensive adaptation is required, the teacher may decide to reject the book. But replacing it may unfortunately not be possible. It might well be the officially adopted text of a ministry of education or school district. Or it might be a recently acquired text in a school that cannot afford a replacement for three more years. Or the deadline may have passed for ordering material for the new school year. In some situations rejecting the language book could mean assuming the responsibility of preparing one's own teaching materials. Anyone who has been through such an experience knows that it is a most difficult, exacting, and time-consuming alternative. A decision to proceed in this direction should not be taken lightly. Circumstances, then, may dictate that even a very unsatisfactory text be adapted.

Broadly speaking, adaptation takes place on three levels: the individualizing of material (expected of all teachers), modifying a text for purposes not intended or anticipated by the author, and compensating for textbook defects. To accomplish his task, the teacher adapter may need to employ one or more of a variety of techniques: supplementing, editing, expanding, personalizing, simplifying, modernizing, localizing, or modifying cultural/situational content. In practice, adaptation may range from extemporaneous oral modification to planned, carefully prepared oral or written supplementation. It can be addressed to problems of lexical expansion, refinement of structural descriptions, provision of readings and drills, alteration of complex structures or older classics as an entrée to their acquisition, or modification of role play or dialog to match the age and vocational interest of students.

THE PRINCIPLE OF CONGRUENCE

Throughout this text, a basic principle will recur in each section and chapter: *Effective adaptation is a matter of achieving "congruence."* The principle of congruence has of course an infinite variety of applications: The poet matches the meter of his poem to his theme; the composer his lyrics and melody. The farmer selects a crop congruent with soil, climate, and market; the industrialist a product compatible with his physical plant and public demand.

The good teacher is likewise constantly striving for congruence among several related variables: teaching materials, methodology, students, course objectives, the target language and its context, and the teacher's own personality and teaching style. We will concentrate on how to achieve congruence between teaching materials—notably the language textbook—and each of the remaining ingredients in the language-learning taxonomy. We will be concerned with such varied matters as textbook congruence with student ability and interests, with teacher background, with the facts of the language as we understand them, with aims of the language program, and with communicating in the real world.

THE SCOPE OF THIS TEXT

Section One deals with achieving congruence between the textbook and the real world. An important aim is to increase student motivation and learning through improved instructional credibility and heightened interest. A second aim is to improve the student's facility in his new language. Chapter 1 concentrates on achieving *language situations* that are relevant and lifelike. Chapter 2 illustrates how *language models* from the textbook can be made appropriate, interesting, and believable. Chapter 3 looks at how *oral communication* can be taught so that it approximates the flow of speech in real-life situations outside the classroom. Adaptation techniques are illustrated by citing examples from textbooks for teaching English as a second language—examples of presentations that we think can be improved. All examples are paraphrased, but each in fact does occur. Since we wish to suggest ways of using and improving textbooks in general, we prefer not to hold up any particular book to criticism.

Section Two deals with congruence in the realm of usage. One aim is to achieve effective language instruction; a corollary aim is to simplify the student's learning task while providing him with accurate language information. Chapter 4 demonstrates how to achieve pedagogical soundness both in exercise work and in basic language presentations. As in Section One, adaptation examples are provided with reference to presentations in contemporary textbooks. In Chapter 5, however, the focus is on the language itself. In seeking congruence with contemporary usage, we look at language surveys instead of drawing upon textbook examples.

Congruence in Section Three applies to variety in language as well as to variety in language learners. One objective is to complement textbook instruction in order that students might utilize the appropriate type of discourse—in short, so that they might communicate more effectively. A second objective is to assist teachers in tailoring instruction to the appropriate student level, thus simplifying the learning task. In Chapter 6, congruence is achieved through the selection of socially appropriate discourse. Chapter 7 is concerned with the more advanced language learners' recognition of language differences reflecting such characteristics as age, sex, and educational background. In Chapter 8, congruence with language proficiency is realized through simplification of reading tasks.

The concluding discussion, in Section Four, illustrates how to achieve congruence pedagogically by adapting the text to match course objectives, variant methodologies, or teaching styles, and how to provide second-language instruction when appropriate materials are unavailable. This section also provides guidance on how to evaluate a text in order to decide where lack of congruence exists and what type of adaptation should be made. Chapter 9 presupposes first, that the teacher plans to evaluate the class textbook; and second, that the teacher will evaluate the teaching situation in order to determine where adaptation is necessary.

Regarding textbook evaluation, our own experience as teachers in a language classroom confirms our conviction that it is not educationally profitable for a teacher to constantly criticize the text he is using, or to harangue its absent author for shortcomings. Excessive criticism may succeed in undermining the students' confidence in the competence of the author but fail to convince the students that the teacher can really do any better. We think a wise teacher will seek in every way possible to cooperate with the author of the book being used. The task becomes one of enlargement or modification, not of criticism and downgrading. Perhaps the most important question in the adaptation of a text for any class is how to establish the cooperation that will yield the most positive results in terms of student learning.

A large number of teachers can be found at the opposite extreme, slavishly "following the book." This text on adaptation is quite obviously of value only to teachers who are interested in assessing their teaching situation and in adjusting their textbook presentation accordingly. Long-range plans for adaptation (the kind that often ultimately lead to the writing of a new, more specific textbook) can be formulated after studying the material in Section Four on textbook evaluation. Further refinement will come as the teacher develops units of instruction or individual lesson plans; and still further modification may be dictated by the dynamics of the actual presentation in the classroom.

Adaptation in Language Teaching could not possibly catalog all needed modifications, but it does attempt to provide examples in the major areas of teaching concern, with the hope that the reader will be able to extrapolate where necessary. The book is intended to be read through, in the order presented; but it is indexed so that it might also serve as a resource text for teachers with varying orientations and needs. For example, it might help the German teacher needing to simplify technical reading materials or the Spanish teacher interested in fostering oral communicative competence, as well as the English-as-a-second-language instructor interested in evaluating specific usage instruction.

The primary audience of *Adaptation* is assumed to be teachers in training, who we feel could profit by adapting specific lessons from sample texts for projected use in hypothetical or real classes. We also feel that teachers in training could benefit from discussing the pedagogical issues implicit in each of the chapters. *Adaptation* is also intended for practicing teachers, teacher interns, administrators, and textbook writers, who might find it helpful as a readily available reference in text selection, curriculum planning, in-service training, and materials production. It is our hope that this book will help the reader not only to utilize the techniques described here but also to develop others of his own that will be suitable for the diverse abilities and needs of the students he serves.

SECTION ONE

CONTEXTUALIZATION:
The Textbook and the Real World

CHAPTER 1

SITUATIONAL REALISM

One of the most popular words in current language-teaching theory is *contextualization*. The idea is associated with cognitive learning patterns, an idea—new but not new—that language should carry a message, should communicate something to somebody. Indeed, in real life the very essence of language is message bearing, transferring information between or among human communicants. And in actual situations the message is always real, genuine communication. In classrooms where we learn to communicate in a second language, messages should whenever possible be real, at least realistic and believable. It is a safe assumption that neither speaker nor hearer will pay significant attention to a message that does not communicate; students, especially, will not concentrate (for very long) on a linguistic form that is devoid of content.

It is of course possible to play language games where communication can be described in terms of scoring points based on manipulation virtuosity (e.g., conundrums, tongue twisters, rhythmic rhymes, pantomime with guessing, imagined situations, etc.), but these activities establish their own context, which can be accepted for the duration of the game. And such game-like activities can be profitably incorporated in language-teaching methodology.

PROVIDING MEANINGFUL PRACTICE:
THREE DIMENSIONS OF REALISM

But actual communication and practice for communication are different matters. Methodologists have recognized the need for oral drills and exercises, for activities that will develop, first of all, the psychomotor coordinations that are inherent in the structure of the target language. Scholars of the audiolingual persuasion have attempted to satisfy this need by providing extensive drills on sentences that are selected because they are useful, logical, typical utterances in the language being learned. By repeating these sentences over and over again until their production becomes smooth, accurate, and unhesitating, the student is expected eventually to achieve mastery of the structure of the language. But repeating the same utterance, with little or no change in the content, probably means that there is a minimum of real communication, especially after the first vocal production. The truly perplexing problem is: How can enough practice be provided to insure learning the physical and psychological coordinations necessary for fluency and still not deny the primary message-carrying function of language use?

Probably some degree of compromise is necessary. If we don't drill we may not learn. But if all we do in our drills is repeat sentences, dialogs, exercises, utterances, etc., we probably won't learn to communicate (Rivers 1972, pp. 71-81). At least, large numbers of students have followed this methodology without developing the desired communication skills. These students sound good when they produce what they have practiced, but they are unable to carry on a meaningful conversation beyond the phatic levels of standard greetings and formula exchanges, and they are not able to comprehend the natural flow of unrehearsed speech when others address them. On the other hand, we cannot merely expose students to language in context and expect them to learn. A form of this methodology was attempted through the grammar-translation-reading methods of the thirties and forties, with singularly undistinguished results. The most promising answer to this dilemma of maximum attention to content with the necessary minimum practice of form is *contextualized practice.* This concept needs to be explained and enlarged.

As we drill, we need to focus on practice activities that are real—or at least seem real. Language-learning materials that have violated this canon have been severely and justifiably criticized. Sentences like *The pen of my maiden aunt lies on the chiffonier* are indeed useless. But this is of course an extreme example: unmarried aunts are not described as *maiden aunts* in the contemporary world, pens don't normally *lie, chiffoniers* are found mainly in antique shops, and in any case would not be a logical place for a pen to be. Not many textbooks in current use offer sentences so transparently meaningless. But there are problems where materials are not ideally suited to teaching real, authentic communication. (Earl Stevick, 1971, uses the terms "strong" and "weak" to contrast useful and relevant language with rare or contrived language. P. 46.)

The most promising answer to the dilemma of providing both communication reality and sufficient practice is materials that reflect an intelligent application of the cognitivist concept of contextualization. If students do in fact have to practice sentences by repeating them, we should recognize that they carry no real message as repetitions; the very least we can do is insist that the message be realistic in as many ways as possible. To this end we offer the first three chapters of this book, each presenting a different aspect of contextualization.

The key word is *realism,* which in the context of a teaching text actually means an artistic approximation to realism. If we were to insist on true reality in speech, with all its false starts, unfinished sentences, restarts, hesitation pauses, fumble words, etc., our teaching materials would be insufferably dull. We can tolerate imperfections when the message is unfolding, but not in the elaboration for exercise and practice. So what we seek to provide is the illusion of reality, in situations that are meaningfully developed and presented in a manner that suggests actual communication.

We see realism in three guises, and we devote a separate chapter to each of the three: situational realism, linguistic realism, and realistic oral interpretation.

This first chapter involves the selection and presentation of realistic events in a compatible setting. There must be a realistic situation in which human interaction takes place. The locale, the participants, the action—all should be consistent with what experience suggests is real for the students who will use the materials. This involves, then, the determination of what events and people will figure in the lessons.

Chapter 2 deals with the selection of the linguistic material, which must be appropriate to the *dramatis personae* and setting of the lesson—and indirectly, of course, to the students. Sentences should be natural, relevant—the things people say when they communicate. (Stevick 1971, p. 53; Bowen in Croft 1972, pp. 409-421.) There must be a consideration of status relationships, style, register, levels, etc.

Chapter 3 is concerned with the actual presentation of the lesson. Assuming the situation is true to life and the language is appropriate, the utterances must then be rendered much as they would be in the real world. Teachers should talk like teachers, children like children—with appropriate age, generational, or sex differences. This is an ambitious effort compared with that undertaken in most traditional classrooms, where nothing but formal classroom language is ever heard or produced. But the price of a simplified school room interpretation is the forfeiting of the opportunity for realistic experience with the actual spoken forms of the language which will prepare students for the complexity of the real world of oral language communication. The place to start a corrective program is before it's needed, i.e., in the beginning language classroom. And there should be a healthy respect for the informal levels of language use that characterize most of the contexts in which we communicate.

The first kind of contextualization, then, involves the physical setting, the second the linguistic selection, and the third the phonological interpretation. All are crucial to the reality of language use, and if any is neglected, all three suffer.

It must be admitted, however, that the theoretical separation of situation, utterance, and pronunciation is not always as neat as an orderly mind might hope. This will become clear as we discuss examples.

ACHIEVING CONGRUENCE
WITH STUDENT INTERESTS

The first area to which contextualization can be applied is the situation. It is logically prior to sentence selection and interpretation, and deficiency in situation is most difficult to remedy. The appropriateness of the situation is, as indicated earlier, closely related to the student group that is to use the materials. The more specifically the group can be identified and described, the more closely the materials can be aimed. In the absence of a particular group of students, materials must be very general and thus risk missing an opportunity for specific relevance.

Note the following dialog:

Stephen: Did you get the classes you wanted?
Phillip: No, I'm stuck with world history and music appreciation.
Stephen: When are they scheduled?
Phillip: World history comes Monday, Wednesday, and Friday at 10:00 a.m., and the music class is Tuesday and Thursday at 8:30.
Stephen: What a drag!
Phillip: Yeah. Can you imagine being in class by 8:30! The only good thing is that I sit right next to a gorgeous redhead named Britt.
Stephen: What'll we do Saturdays and Sundays?
Phillip: There are always football games and fraternity dances on weekends.
Stephen: I sure hope I can get into Alpha Kappa Gamma.
Phillip: Well, see you later. I've got to go to the library and study.

Stephen:	Are you sure it's not to see Britt?
Phillip:	No, I don't know her well enough yet.

This dialog is not in any case too attractive as an example of human experience, though it might be satisfactory for students in secondary school or at the lower division university level, where concern for class schedules, dating, fraternity affiliation, athletic competition, etc., are matters of general interest; in addition, the level of expression is quite appropriate to this age group and to the formality level of the occasion. But it would be clearly inappropriate in a class where adults are learning a second language for professional purposes. And this is the most difficult kind of deficiency to remedy, since the lesson presentation introduces the ideas, concerns, and vocabulary that reenter in drills and in later lessons. A teacher should have these considerations very much in mind when the text is selected. If an age mismatch cannot be avoided, it is generally better that young students should pretend they are older than that older learners pretend they are young.

But assuming the choice of textbook has been made and can't be changed, what can a teacher do with a text of this kind that is not written to the age level of the students? We suggest using the original dialog for a brief vocabulary presentation, since the words subsequently appear in later lessons, but then immediately going to a supplementary dialog, rewritten to include at least some of the same ideas and words, but aimed at the proper age level:

Stanley:	May I show you around the office?
Peter:	Yes thanks. When do we have staff meet-
ings?	
Stanley:	Tuesdays at 10:00 a.m. They're usually
short.	
Peter:	Who's that good looking girl?
Stanley:	Oh that's Britt. She's one of the aides.
Peter:	Does the office have a library?
Stanley:	Yes, a small one. But it's strong on eco-
nomics.	
Peter:	Can we come in on weekends?

> *Stanley*:   Yes, you'll get a building key. I occasion-
> nally work on Saturday or Sunday.
> *Peter*:   Well, thanks. I may have some more ques-
> tions later.

There is only a partial overlap, and some new words have crept in. The student will likely remember the ones that are useful to him, and if he doesn't learn all the original or the additional ones it's not serious. Native speakers rarely learn all the words they are exposed to the first time they hear them. If words are important they'll be back. Note that only three days of the week are mentioned in the supplement though all seven were presented in the original. In drills the other weekdays can be substituted for *Tuesday* as the day for staff meetings.

Just forget the dating, fraternities, course schedules, etc., unless the mature students show some special interest. And later on, in drill sentences, either drop sentences with references to uninteresting details, or change dates to conferences, football games to professional conventions, etc. As we said, it's not easy to accommodate poorly fitting situational materials, but it can be done, and generally the effort is worthwhile.

SELECTING PROBABLE SITUATIONS

Sometimes the situational misfit is due to a curriculum committee's desire to combine language learning with good citizenship or character development. The result is a cast of goody-goody characters incapable of acting like real humans.

Note the following dialog:

> *Pablo*:   Where's Mother?
> *Ana*:   Mother's gone to the market.
> *David*:   Oh fine! That means she'll buy us some good
> food.
> *Maria*:   What shall we do while she's gone?
> *Rosa*:   I know! Let's surprise her and clean the house.
> *David*:   What a fine idea! I'll dust the furniture.
> *Ana*:   Good. I'll sweep the floor.

Pedro: Fine. I'll wash the windows.
Maria: I'll wash the dishes.
Rosa: I'll make the beds.
Ana: Baby brother can pick up his toys.
Pablo: Won't Mother be happy when she comes home!
David: Yes, and how good we'll all feel!

This dialog manages to present the relevant vocabulary for housekeeping, though the subject itself is probably of limited interest to children. And however well-intentioned the effort to make the students better members of their families, the result will probably be boredom. This is not a picture of the real world seen through a child's eyes.

This dialog can be improved somewhat by eliminating the most unrealistic elements:

Pablo: Where's Mother?
Ana: She's gone to the market, and she says we have
    to clean the house.
David: Again? It's always dirty.
Ana: Maybe so. Anyway, everybody take a slip of
    paper out of this hat. It will say what you have to do.

Maria: I sweep the floor.
Rosa: I wash the dishes.
David: Darn it. I have to wash windows. Anyone want
    to trade?
Pedro: I make the beds.
Ana: And Carlitos, you pick up your toys.

The changes are minimal and worth making, especially since the materials seem to be designed for younger children, who could be expected to concentrate on the spoken language.

One could say that the revision above is really linguistic. So it is, in part. But the situation is changed, too, from an unnatural script that emphasizes unlikely initiative to a more probable context of imposed responsibilities. Changing the situation will of course almost always have an effect on the linguistic exchanges that actualize the situation.

The examples so far have been concerned with dialogs and more specifically with lesson presentations. But situational realism can be applied to drill sections as well. Note the following drill sequence introduced by illustrations of several adults holding lighted matches:

> If James isn't careful, he'll burn himself.
> James will burn himself if he isn't careful.
> If Elizabeth isn't careful, she'll burn herself.
> Elizabeth will burn herself if she isn't careful.
> If Edward and Penelope aren't careful, they'll burn themselves.
> Edward and Penelope will burn themselves if they aren't careful.

A very simple way to improve this drill is to substitute pictures of children for those of adults holding matches. Possibly names with diminutive endings would be more appropriate as

reference to children: Jimmy, Betty, Eddie, and Penny for James, Elizabeth, Edward, and Penelope. The context is immediately made more realistic and therefore more acceptable. We will return to this drill situation in the next chapter with further suggestions for expansion in an enlarged context.

One of the erstwhile popular approaches to language teaching specifies a presentation that attempts to unite word with action in a close-knit sequence. The purpose is admirable, but the result leaves much to be desired. Here's a sample lesson segment:

Phase I   *Instructor*:   Walk around this desk.
Instructor: (*While walking*) I'm walking around this desk.
(Several repetitions while students observe and listen)

Phase II   *Instructor*:   Walk around this desk.
Students: (*Repeating orally*) Walk around this desk.
Instructor: What are you doing?
Students: What are you doing?
Instructor: (*Walking*) I'm walking around this desk.
Students: (*Seated*) I'm walking around this desk.

Phase III   Instructor conducts dialog with individual students.

Phase IV   Students alternate conducting dialog drill with each other in pairs. (Students go through actual actions in Phases III and IV.)

The drill has some good points. It is simple and teachable in its present form. It involves actions and speech in an illustrative relationship. But it is unnecessarily artificial in several respects: an instructor asking himself questions in a conversation where he takes both parts, both instructor and students asking and answering their own questions, violating the "truth factor" by having students claim to be executing actions which they in fact are observing someone else perform. The weakest aspect is probably the situation itself: people don't ask as a means of learning what they can observe directly, especially when the activities queried are simple and transparent.

One small modification of procedure that would improve this drill is to have it presented by two people, with an aide or a student helping the teacher. Then one could query and one answer, which is the normal way questions are asked and answered. In all cases, only "performers" should claim to be doing an action. If this means risking chaos and loss of discipline by having everybody in the room walking around desks, other relatively more subdued actions can be substituted, such as students holding up a book, standing by their desk, raising both arms, reading their English book, writing their name, etc. There remains the illogicality of the same person requesting an action and then inquiring about it. This can be remedied by a device that is enormously useful and productive in many phases of language teaching: indirect commands. The teacher relays some or all of his instructions and questions through another person, a student. Note the following format:

Teacher:	Abdul, ask Ahmed to hold his book up.
Abdul:	Ahmed, hold your book up.
Ahmed:	(*complies*)
Teacher:	Mona, ask Ahmed what he's doing.
Mona:	What are you doing, Ahmed?
Teacher:	(*if necessary*) Answer, Ahmed.
Ahmed:	I'm holding my book up.
Teacher:	What's he doing, Mona?
Mona:	He's holding his book up.
Teacher:	Is that right, Abdul?
Abdul:	Yes, that's right.

This device doesn't turn a dull lesson into a fascinating experience, but it does correct some of the blatant weaknesses. Also, it makes the pretense necessary to carry out this kind of oral exchange just a little easier. Additionally, it would be relatively simple, if the class is at an appropriate stage, to expand this -*ing*-form question to refer to the future, using an adverb in the question *What are you doing this afternoon/ tonight/tomorrow?* and an answer framed with *going to*: *I'm going to read a book/see a movie/visit my grandmother.* These answers, if needed, can be cued by indirect instruction, by a stage whisper, or by an honest-to-goodness private whisper. Often this latter procedure will generate a little interest among other students, as the language functions in its normal role: communicating something they don't already know.

One important application of situational realism is in the realm of attitude. We once saw a French FLES class (foreign language in the elementary schools) where third graders were practicing introduction formulas that specified the children's production of *Bonjour, monsieur*; *Bonjour, mademoiselle* while they shook hands and bowed stiffly from the waist. This is wrong in English and wrong in French; children don't behave in this way. The implication that this is the "French" way is misleading; and worse, it reinforces the stereotype that French people are somehow effeminate and unnatural.

Could the lesson which uses walking around the desk be salvaged by insuring that nobody reports doing something unless he is actually doing it? Probably not. Under normal circumstances people just don't go around announcing what they're doing. That isn't to say that such an activity must be rigorously excluded from a classroom. It can be used, and the resilience of the students will assure no permanent damage is done. (Students have a considerably large capacity to absorb nonsense.) But a lesson sequence should not be limited to such a simple routine, even in an elementary lesson. This is a general principle of inestimable value: Lessons may incorporate manipulative activities, but they should always aim at real communication as the culmination (Prator 1965). We can see the value of a lesson which ends as follows (cf. Paulston 1970, p. 192):

Teacher:	What are you doing?
Student:	I'm reading a book.
Teacher:	Are you really?
Student:	No, not really.
Teacher:	What *are* you doing?
Student:	I'm answering your questions.
Teacher:	Good. Very good.

Methodologists have talked at considerable length about "truth value." Some have suggested that in the early stages of a course, when students are limited to a few identification frames, only teachers should say *I am a teacher* and only students should say *I am a student.* The reason cited is that we should respect the truth. But this inflicts severe limitations that may not really be necessary. Even literal-minded children can project onto this structure the meaning *I want to pretend I am a* _____. To exclude any sentence that is not literally true is an unimaginative application of the truth-value concept.

One situation drill comes to mind that has been encouraged, if not suggested, by the linguists whose theories and descriptions have had a notable effect on language teaching. Somehow the theorists decided that statements are organizationally simpler than questions, and that it is therefore descriptively more efficient to derive questions from statements than vice versa. This may indeed well be. But the illogical application to language classes has been to start with statements and produce the questions which would elicit or at least explain the statements. This is totally the reverse of real-life experience, where questions are only asked if the answers are not yet available. Note the following drill, which is accompanied by a sketch of a family at an airport:

1. Mr. Adams had a nice
   flight.   Did he have a nice flight?

2. The Wilsons had a
   wonderful trip.   _____ ?

3. Marilyn had a good time
   at the dance.   _____ ?

4. The secretaries had a
   grand vacation.   _____ ?

5. Jim and you had an
   exciting Fair.   _____ ?

The lack of any contextualization (beyond the picture which applies only to the first sentence) compounds the unnatural sequencing of answer-question. One wants to say, "Well yes, dummy; didn't you hear me say so?" Virtually no understanding of the sentences is necessary to perform this exercise correctly; the student who knows the rudiments of number and gender juggles the words to fit the pattern. There is little or no communication involved. And the sentences in the drill are not related to each other in any logical way, not even suggestively. They are simply a miscellaneous collection of utterances. The last one is even unidiomatic, unless hosting instead of attending is the expected interpretation, which the unexpected capitalization makes unlikely. This would be a good item to skip—even to ask students to cross out.

A related problem is common in drills for negation. We are told to start with the model sentence *George is my brother* and apply the cue "Negate" to produce *George is not my brother.* With such a contradiction one wants to ask, "Well is he or isn't he?" Both of these problems can be handled quite readily by a change in reference. Questions *can* follow statements if they don't query exactly the same information given:

Mr. Adams had a nice flight.	Did Mrs. Adams have a nice flight, too?
The Wilsons had a wonderful trip.	Did the Taylors have a wonderful trip, too?

Using this approach with affirmative-negative practice, we have:

George is my brother.	But Harold isn't my brother; he's my cousin.
Robert is my uncle.	But Fred isn't my uncle; he's my godfather.

The question that immediately queries information just given can also be contextualized by employing an echo question:

Mr. Adams had a nice flight.	(Did you say) Mr. Adams had a nice flight?
The Wilsons went to Guatemala.	The Wilsons went to Guatemala? *or* Where did you say the Wilsons went? *or* Where did the Wilsons go?

The echo question, pronounced on very high and rising pitch, asks for confirmation of information that may not have been accurately heard. The expression *did you say* can be optionally added to increase realism. (This special question form is of course not the neutral pattern that would normally be taught first to a class.)

Again, a promising solution for a contextualized presentation is directed questions:

Teacher:	Audra, ask Joel if Mr. Adams had a nice flight.
Audra:	Joel, did Mr. Adams have a nice flight?
Teacher:	Joel, tell her he certainly did.
Joel:	He certainly did.
Teacher:	Audra, ask him where Mr. Adams went.
Audra:	Where did he go?
Teacher:	Joel, answer.
Joel:	I don't know.
Teacher:	What did he say, Audra?
Audra:	He says he doesn't know.
Teacher:	Tell him to ask Mr. Adams. Kevin you be Mr. Adams.
Audra:	Ask Kevin. I mean ask Mr. Adams.
Joel:	Mr. Adams, where did you go?
Teacher:	Kevin, give him an answer Make it up.
Kevin:	I went to Guatemala.
Teacher:	Audra, ask Joel what he said.
Audra:	What did Mr. Adams say, Joel?
Joel:	He said he went to Guatemala.

Any time the exchange generates enough interest to continue on its own, the teacher can fade into the background and wait until a further prompt or a new idea is needed. Imagination is the source, but artistic realism is the means.

Situational realism, or the contextualization that deals with locale and setting, is the first requisite of any aspect of a lesson. There must be a believable illusion of real people participating in plausible interactions, situations that students of whatever age and background can identify themselves with. This seems to mean that different kinds of student groups need different sets of materials, and this is probably a pedagogical ideal. A considerable amount of adjustment, however, can be made by the sensitive and alert teacher to "customize" any text to a particular class. Suggestions on how to do this will be elaborated in the next chapter.

CHAPTER 2
LINGUISTIC REALISM

Once the setting in a language lesson is a satisfactory example of a normal human relationship, the next question to be dealt with is the content and form of the communication. Do participants' interactions represent realistic exchanges of information? Do they make statements and offer reactions that convincingly reflect the personalities and situations involved? In other words, is the language of the lesson realistic? Are the sentences that were selected to present the lesson appropriate to the situations, so the lesson can successfully be contextualized?

LINGUISTIC REALISM
IN LESSON PRESENTATIONS

In evaluating naturalness of expression, the teacher may find textbook lessons with examples of language use that just do not represent the real world. People interacting in real life situations would not use the utterances assigned to them in the lessons. The following example dialog is situationally acceptable. People do travel and make friends that they remember. But would they talk about it in the following way?

> *Jack*:　　Do you know anybody in Los Angeles, Fred?
> *Fred*:　　Yes. I know a lot of people in Los Angeles.
> *Jack*:　　Do you know anybody in Moscow?

Fred: Yes, I do. I know quite a few people in Moscow.
Jack: Do you know anyone in Calcutta?
Fred: Yes, I do. I have several friends in Calcutta.
Jack: Fred, how much do you weigh?
Fred: I'd rather not tell my weight.
Jack: Good-bye, Fred. I must go now.
Fred: Good-bye, Jack. See you next week.

This dialog is not hard to criticize. There is no motivation suggested for the series of questions on friends around the world. But the question on weight is *really* odd. What does Fred's weight have to do with the world of friendship? And why does Fred so strangely decline to answer? Then the conversation is abruptly broken off, almost suggesting sudden disenchantment. To the experienced teacher it looks like the author expected to need the verb *weigh* for some purpose, so stuck it in, regardless of what it did to the plausibility of the dialog presentation.

The dialog is not wholly without merit. It is short and simple, so can be learned easily; it is reasonably idiomatic, including short-form responses that are characteristic of conversation; it provides practice with questions and answers and presents several useful pre-determiners appropriate for use with count nouns (*a lot of, a few, several*). But it sounds like an interrogation. One person does all the questioning and the other all the answering. The questions sound improbable and the answers unlikely. The sequence is repetitive and mechanical, with no link between exchanges. The question on weight is not only impertinent, but also surprisingly out of context.

What can be done to improve this lesson? Obviously the language used must be congruent with the language in the real world. An important and simple modification is to eliminate from the dialog the question on weight. If *weigh* is needed, and an appropriate dialog context would take too much space and time at this point, better just introduce it in the drills where it is needed. The rest of the dialog can be brightened up, perhaps taking some such form as the following:

Jack: What a wonderful vacation!
Fred: Yes. London, Athens, and Cairo are my favor-
    ite cities.

Jack: Do you know anybody in London?
Fred: Yes, I know a lot of people there.
Jack: Oh? Do you know anyone in Athens?
Fred: Yes, I do. I know quite a few people there, too.
Jack: Well. How about Cairo?
Fred: I have several very good friends at the university there.
Jack: Boy, you get around.

The dialog is no longer; in fact it's a little shorter. Lopping off the good-byes is no loss, since contexts for learning greetings and leavetakings are never missing. The dialog now sounds more like an exchange between real people. Except for the stative verb *weigh*, all of the grammar of the original is retained, so students will be just as ready for grammar practice. Most important, it should be possible to retain student attention better with a more plausible and realistic dialog.

LINGUISTIC REALISM IN LANGUAGE PRACTICE

While a measure of situational reality can quite legitimately be expected in a dialog that introduces new patterns, students and teachers are usually less demanding of the sentences and situations that make up drill sequences, where a major goal may be accurate kinesthetic manipulation and familiarization with an important basic sentence pattern. Still, there may be opportunities to inject more reality and variety into practice sessions without losing the benefit of practice. Indeed, if the drill segment of the lesson can be made more interesting, assimilation of the patterns presented may come sooner and more effectively.

In Chapter 1 we cited a drill sequence based on the danger of getting burned if one plays with matches. (*If Jimmy isn't careful, he'll burn himself; Jimmy will burn himself if he isn't careful*; etc.) We called attention to the possibility of improving the lesson by selecting participants who fit the situation more appropriately: children rather than adults. Now we would like to show how this situation can be enlarged to profitably extend the semantic coverage of the concept *burn*.

In its original form the drill has some useful features: it presents a representative sample of third-person reflexive pronouns and the optional positions of *if*-clauses. The sentences are also reasonably idiomatic. But it has weaknesses. The repetition of the particular sentence pattern is not at all motivated. And the drill is remote from bona fide communication, unnecessarily bland semantically and culturally—the sort of activity that can lead to "structural hypnosis." Some genuine and more realistic variation could be provided by introducing situations to expand the semantic range of *burn*. Simple stick-figure drawings (see illustrations) can cue drill sentences. All are situations that will likely be familiar to students. In fact, this is what good drills *should* do—enrich the application of the drill sentences to show the extent of the conceptual coverage.

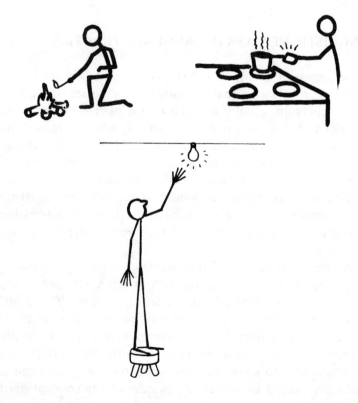

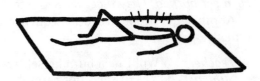

With the drawings to set the context, questions can serve as further cues:

Teacher: What will happen to Leo if he's not careful, Ahmed?
Ahmed: He'll burn himself.
Teacher: If Lucia's not careful, what will happen to her, Boris?
Boris: She'll burn herself.

It's a short step to cueing both the question and the answer with directed instructions:

Teacher: Gaya, ask Mona what will happen to Antonio if . . .
Gaya: Mona, what will happen to Antonio if he's not careful?
Mona: He'll burn himself.
Teacher: Jan, ask Hilda what will happen to Fernando and Maria if . . .
Jan: Hilda, what will happen to Fernando and Maria if they're not careful?
Hilda: They'll burn themselves.

If the students can handle the vocabulary (and perhaps even if some of them can't—unless the lesson is already lexically overloaded), we'd be tempted to interject an occasional *Why?* after a declaration that someone will burn himself. With an occasional cue if needed, some class members can be expected to say *Because the fire/bulb/oven/sun is hot.* This is a timely reminder that effects normally have causes and that cause and effect relationships should be borne in mind in making explanations of physical events. Unless the grammar content of the lesson is heavy, it would also be justifiable to introduce the very useful paraphrase "get burned," even if only as a preliminary exposure to a later more thorough presentation: *He'll get burned/They'll get burned,* etc.

Another question-cued drill sequence could be built on the reflexive pattern:

Teacher: Will Lucia burn herself (get burned)?
Student: Yes, if she's not careful.

This can be expanded and elaborated on by a very simple additional instruction:

Teacher: Tell Jorge.
Student: Lucia will burn herself (get burned) if she's not careful.
Teacher: Thank you. Jim, what will happen to Fernando and Maria if they're not careful?
Jim: They'll burn themselves (get burned).
Teacher: Good, tell Dennis.
Jim: If they're not careful, Fernando and Maria will burn themselves (get burned).

This is of course not really communication. It's a language game played for the sake of practice. But with good will and an occasional knowing smile, it can serve as a reasonable substitute, especially if changes are introduced to avoid extended verbatim repetition with no variation except the voice of a different student.

In some drill sequences there is apparently no thought at all of a situation; all is subordinated to the presentation or practice of a paradigm. The following sample is illustrative:

Directions: Look at the pictures and chart. Give appropriate sentences to go with the words *I, you, he,* etc.

Subj.	Obj.	Preposed poss.	Postposed poss.
I	me	my	mine
you	you	your	yours
he	him	his	his
she	her	her	hers
it	it	its	—
we	us	our	ours
they	them	their	theirs

You bought a knife. It's yours. It's your knife. If you're careful, you won't cut yourself.

We bought a knife. It's ours. It's our knife. If we're careful, we won't cut ourselves.

He bought a knife. It's his. It's his knife. If he's careful, he won't cut himself.

These sentences are not only boring and mechanical but also choppy and artificial. Particularly distressing is the patterned repetition of the information about possession, as if the speaker felt he couldn't be believed: *It's yours. It's your knife.* The problem is finding an effective way of practicing the *my/mine* types of possessive pronouns, a situation that can at least to some extent be contextualized. This can be done without relying on the objectionable *my/mine* juxtaposition in unmotivated, redundant sentences. The following sequence is somewhat less mechanical.

Teacher:	Whose pen is this?
Student:	It's mine. My mother gave it to me.
Teacher:	Whose car is this?
Student:	It's mine. My father gave it to me.
Teacher:	Whose coat is this?
Student:	It's hers. Her mother bought it for her.

My/mine, her/hers, etc., can thus be introduced and drilled without the overly conspicuous sequencing of the two forms in sentences conveying exactly the same information.

If this drill should follow somewhere close behind the *burn himself* drill discussed earlier, it might be productive to echo that drill, provide a review practice for reflexive pronouns, and tie the two ideas together by emphasizing the pattern components they have in common.

Teacher: Bobby, if you're not careful with that knife, what will happen?
Bobby: I'll cut myself.
Teacher: Jerry, if Bobby's not careful with his knife, what will happen?
Jerry: He'll cut himself.
Teacher: Tell Lonny.
Jerry: If Bobby's not careful with his knife, he'll cut himself.
Teacher: Betty, if Bobby *is* careful with his knife, what won't happen?
Betty: He won't cut himself.
Teacher: Tell Eileen.
Betty: If Bobby's careful with his knife, he won't cut himself.

ACCEPTING INFORMAL LANGUAGE

Occasionally the situation set for a lesson segment is natural and realistic, but the text author or curriculum writer makes some restrictive linguistic assumptions that damage realism and make meaningful contextualization difficult or impossible. One of these practices is based on the assumption that the standard contractions of English are somehow deficient linguistic expressions which should be avoided. In formal writing the absence of contracted forms is common practice, but introduced into stories which present dialog—especially with children as participants—the result is devastating. Note the following exchange:

Where is Jonathan? He is coming with us, is he not?
Yes, he is coming. Let us get ready to go.

This is not the way children talk—or anyone else. In one project that we consulted for some years ago, our greatest success was convincing a team of authors that contractions are real and should be recognized, especially in dialog sentences spoken by children. But even so we had to compromise: the first occurrence of any contractable combination was presented uncontracted, after which the contraction was allowed. The stories began to sound much more natural as the reader got past these first occurrences. The teacher would be well advised to adapt such material so that her students will encounter contractions from the outset. Students should recognize that contractions are normally appropriate in speech and even in informal writing. The more rare uncontracted form (*He* is *at home*) can be introduced later when instruction in contradictions and contrastive stress is appropriate.

Why do authors feel they should avoid contractions? Probably for a combination of reasons: their use is felt to be careless and substandard; there is a tradition that while the oral language can't really avoid contractions, they should not be recognized and dignified in writing; schools, it is felt, are obligated to observe and encourage the highest standards. And indeed, even for English-speaking children, there is a kind of storytelling style that attempts to "upgrade" language use by employing excessively formal devices such as the avoidance of contractions, the observance of certain of the "etiquette rules" of grammar (no prepositions at the end of sentences, no split infinitives, careful observance of the so-called traditional rules for *shall* and *will*, etc.—see "Old Wives Tales" in Chapter 5). This does little harm to native English-speaking children, except for advancing the mild deception that a special style and grammar will be needed if one is to become a good storyteller. But it can be very prejudicial to a second-language student whose main contact with English is through the language classes of the schools. The selection of linguistic material should embody, not exclude, the forms of normal expression. Otherwise a stumbling block is placed in the path of the child who must relearn forms properly contracted or forever suffer the penalty of diminished efficiency of communication.

Certainly, informal language should not be neglected as a result of the teacher's concentration on the seldom used formal forms of expression. Ideally both would ultimately be presented if a well-rounded education is intended, but informal expression should in our opinion be given priority in both time and selection, since informal language use plays such a predominant role in communication. Formal expression can come later, if and when needed, just as it does in the education of native speakers. If we deny this conclusion, we may be on the way to producing still another generation of linguistic cripples.

Another defect of linguistic expression can be seen in the specification of full-sentence responses to questions, a practice not at all uncommon among language teachers and textbook writers. The following exercise is typical of this attitude.

Directions: Answer each of the following questions in a complete sentence beginning with *yes* or *no*.

1. Did Artur Rubinstein's family object to his playing the piano?

   No, Artur Rubinstein's family did not object to his playing the piano.

2. Did they object to his composing music?

   _____

3. Did they object to his traveling abroad?

   _____

4. Did the American people have the privilege of hearing him perform first?

   _____

5. Did the Russian people have the privilege of hearing him perform in Moscow?

   _____

This is part of a longer exercise designed to provide review in answering questions and to provide controlled practice in using "prepositions determined by the preceding word." The cultural-semantic content is substantive and of probable interest to mature students. The questions throughout the exercise are on the same topic and are rather closely linked to each other; this should help students to become involved in the subject rather than simply reciting grammatical structures. The prepositions are featured in more than one context in order to enhance understanding.

One weakness in this exercise involving prepositions is that the author inadvertently mixes dissimilar grammatical constructions: the two-word verb, and prepositions controlled by a preceding noun, constructions which have different junctural features. The pronunciation contrast between the two forms must be recognized and taught. While neglecting the pronunciation contrast is not a terrible mistake, a more serious pedagogical criticism of the original drill is that the dynamic or productive activity is limited to the transformation of a question to a statement; the only "preposition" training is the passive copying of the preposition and its governing word.

But the primary weakness is the requirement to answer in complete sentences, a specification apparently laid on to insure that students practice the prepositions. But this encourages them to do precisely what they would not do: provide an invariable, automatic, mechanical iteration of the full question in the response. Students should rather be encouraged to use short-form responses, as speakers in natural circumstances invariably do. But some teachers feel the full-sentence answer is the best solution to the problem of providing occasions where full sentences should be used. Otherwise student participation is limited to *Yes ma'am, No sir, Yes, it is, No, they haven't,* etc.

This is surely the wrong solution. If full-sentence practice is needed, there are adequate and much more natural procedures of elicitation. One is the use of diverse-answer questions which must be replied to with full-sentence responses: Are you coming to the class picnic or do you still have that babysitting job? Another solution is the use of directed dialogs, by means of which ample practice in producing any kind of sentence can be provided:

Teacher: Ben, ask Nita what she knows about Leonard Bernstein.

Ben: Nita, what do you know about Leonard Bernstein?

Teacher: Nita, tell Ben "Not too much," and that "he was an American composer, wasn't he?"
Nita: Not too much. He was an American composer, wasn't he?
Teacher: Ben, say "yes," and tell her he wrote "West Side Story." But tell her, too, that he was also famous as a conductor.
Ben: Yes, he wrote "West Side Story," but he was also famous as a conductor.
Teacher: Nita, ask Ben, "A conductor of what?"
Nita: A conductor of what?
Teacher: Ben, say "Of a symphony orchestra! Of the New York Philharmonic Orchestra."
Ben: Of a symphony orchestra, of the New York Philharmonic Orchestra.
Teacher: Nita, tell Ben you really liked the movie "West Side Story."
Nita: I really liked the movie "West Side Story."
Teacher: Ben, tell Nita you did too, and that you agree with Bernstein that theater music will become popular in the future.
Ben: Well, I did too. I agree with Bernstein that theater music will become popular in the future.

With this type of guidance students can be led to produce statements, questions, short answers, rejoinders, or any other form of the spoken language; and these structures can be readily mixed to produce a very natural sounding conversation. And not the least of its virtues is that this is student-to-student conversation, from which the teacher can retreat any time the students give evidence of being able to continue on their own.

One feature that makes full-sentence answers a bit risky, unless they are thoroughly presented in various contrasting contexts, is that such a response can readily be interpreted as an expression of annoyance:

Did you pass the test?
Yes, I passed the test! (Didn't you think I could?)

An "emphatic" answer (*Yes, I passed the test! Isn't that great!*) has to be produced with a compatible intonation pattern. If a neutral response is desired, the full-sentence response should be avoided in order not to convey one of the "special" interpretations just referred to.

INTRODUCING SOCIALLY APPROPRIATE EXCHANGES

So much for full-sentence responses. We turn now to even subtler matters related to appropriate context. Such problems are likely to occur in more advanced classes. Consider the following pattern by which a drill is introduced:

Teacher	*Student*
George was certainly drunk last night.	Oh, I didn't notice.
She always comes in late, doesn't she?	Oh, is that so?
It seems he's always grouchy on Monday mornings.	_____
Most Americans are prejudiced against people with a foreign accent.	_____
West-coast ball clubs can't stand up to those from the East.	_____
Which presidential candidate would you vote for if you were an American citizen?	_____

This is a well-conceived communicative drill for practicing the desirable skill of offering a noncommittal response or comment. It shows how to respond discreetly to a personal or loaded utterance and demonstrates effectively that statements as well as questions usually require some acknowledgment. It is natural, idiomatic, and adequately open-ended.

But there are two possible difficulties: the *purpose* has to be inferred and students are not invited to develop other alternative responses. The problem is compounded since neither suggested response fits all the situations implied by the subsequent stimulus sentences (e.g., the last sentence). Often, if the purpose is not explicitly understood, students move perfunctorily through a sequence, only dimly surmising the real communication function of the pattern.

One of the advantages that cognitive theory offers, particularly to mature, adult students, is the legitimacy of an explanation regarding how and why pieces of a communicative exchange are put together. The present drill could helpfully be introduced by a problem-solving discussion to arouse interest and show the relevance and value of the exercise as a means to build a reservoir of responses which would appropriately allow a communicant to signal that he is attentive and listening, but without expressing concurrence or disagreement.

As an example of an occasion when a noncommittal response is appropriate, a setting can be offered as follows: "You are a foreign student riding with your American host and hostess when the latter chides her husband for being careless in almost striking a boy on a bicycle. The host disagrees, saying it was the boy's fault. The hostess (rather tactlessly) asks you to agree with her accusation. What do you say?" From such problem-solving discussions and/or role play, appropriate responses associated with specific situations can be generated, such as *I guess I really wasn't watching.* Here are sample neutral responses for other "loaded" situations:

I didn't know that.
Well, what do you know?
Do you think so?

A student can learn to be sympathetic, but still noncommittal, with responses such as

That doesn't surprise me at all.
I guess I've got a lot to learn.
You don't say.

As many of these alternatives as possible should be drawn from class members, verified or modified by the instructor.

This kind of activity could be expanded in subsequent lessons to explore situations that call for mild approval, strong approval, mild disapproval, or strong disapproval, also stressing the status of communicants (friend, child, teacher, employer, stranger, etc.) and the setting or occasion (informal conversation, committee meeting, invitation to a friend's parents' home, news interview, etc.). It would be appropriate to reintroduce this exercise from time to time to confirm responses and increase one's repertoire of rejoinders.

Of course rejoinders must be taught with care, to assure that they are used appropriately. If a student's teacher asks why an assignment was not turned in, an answer like *I'll bring it when it's ready* is not appropriate. Or if the principal sees a student in the hall during a class hour and asks what class he should be in, an answer like *Who wants to know?* would probably spell trouble. Two textbooks of this decade include a number of exercises which focus on highly informal and even slangy rejoinders such as *Are you kidding?*, *So what?*, and *No way*, but with little or no comment on when such expressions are appropriate. Naturally the rejoinders have to fit the situations, or communicative competence is not promoted. It is part of the responsibility of the teacher and textbook to teach *when* it is appropriate to use the various items that are taught.

The lessons to be learned from this chapter are: (1) that situational reality can be improved in dialogs or other contexts which presume to show real people communicating, (2) that a drill sequence can often be modified in the direction of more realistic communication, (3) that at a more advanced level realistic elements of communication, including informal usage, should be generously introduced in drill activities, and (4) that drills should as much as possible fit the social situation. Often in a drill context it is easier to modify the situation than to change the order of structural points introduced. Of course some textbook situations are so bland or contrived that it is almost impossible to reconstruct a drill using life-like communication. One final suggestion for the teacher—one that will assure his continuing superiority to a tape playback or other teaching machine—is that occasionally, and especially if students are nodding or inattentive, he should do something unexpected. If this unexpected move, or statement, or question, can somehow be related to the point under treatment, so much the better.

CHAPTER 3
REALISTIC ORAL INTERPRETATION

With a satisfactory setting and a selection of utterances that appropriately and convincingly develop the lesson situations, the next requirement is a satisfactory oral interpretation of the lesson. As most students know from personal experience, even well-conceived lessons often seem to lack relevance and interest because of inappropriate oral rendition in the classroom. Almost all vestiges of real people communicating in normal and natural ways can be lost.

The burden of oral interpretation falls most heavily on the teacher, since text authors can, if they wish, avoid dealing with such problems as the pronunciation of words in context. In fact many texts say little or nothing about pronunciation in any form, retreating to the safety of standard orthography, apparently feeling that oral interpretation is somebody else's responsibility. Or pronunciation, if treated, is given a cursory item-by-item presentation, for the most part neglecting what really happens in the stream of speech when people actually communicate. The result has often been a monotonous classroom style with no richness or depth to match the sociolinguistic nuances that language in real life must interpret. Unfortunately, the result has been students that can't communicate satisfactorily—even after years of instruction.

Given the classroom prejudices that exist against real speech in everyday situations, perhaps criticisms of text writers should be muted a bit. They present their material in written form, and there are some very strong traditions, many quite arbitrary, that they have to accept or at their peril reject. Rejection means conflict with an unseen audience and the risk that the book may not be selected for use. A minor example is the acceptability (at an appropriate style level) in written English of the contraction *there's* from *there is*, but the somewhat strange rejection of the plural equivalent: *there're* is not admissible as an expression of *there are*. From the point of view of the spoken language this is certainly inconsistent since both contractions are equally natural, with pronunciations /dhɛrz/ and /dhɛ́rər/.[1] A text author would almost have to be an evangelist to be willing to question the propriety of the conventions of the written language. So, rather than take the chance of authoring a book that is little used, he conforms to the somewhat narrow strictures of convention.

As a result, pronunciation has come to be a rather specialized field, with such pronunciation instruction as is given relegated to a special isolated part of the class hour. Not infrequently nowadays many teachers tell themselves that adequate pronunciation can be acquired through osmosis, and they therefore largely ignore systematic instruction in pronunciation. Under these circumstances it is not surprising that pronunciation is rarely contextualized in lesson presentations.

THE SCOPE OF THE PROBLEM

If pronunciation is to be left as a special responsibility of the teacher, the more reason the teacher must be ready to perform acceptably. This means having information and (if not a native speaker) skills adequate for the assignment, but perhaps more important, an understanding and appreciation of the scope of the problems. The textbook author, by respecting the conventions, can avoid such problems as variation based on dialect— geographic or social. Is *water* to be pronounced /wɑ́tər/ or /wɔ́tər/ or /wɔ́tə/? The spelling *water* is conveniently neutral, but the teacher has to say *something* if the language is to have any aural reality.

An even more perplexing problem is what to do about the variations that characterize pronunciation in the flow of speech. In many dictionaries the prepositions *for* and *to* are listed with the pronunciations /fɔr/ and /tuw/, and these indeed are the normal pronunciations of the words in isolation. But this information doesn't take into account the fact that in a great majority of occurrences in sentence contexts the normal pronunciations are /fər/ and /tə/. The spelling doesn't contain this information, and general textbooks rarely do; so if the teacher neglects to present the authentic pattern, the students will internalize habits that include /fɔr/ and /tuw/. This is regrettable but not pedagogically crucial, since other speakers will understand—and tolerance for improperly accented speech is generally high. The real misfortune is that the students will not be able to understand other speakers, unless a special schoolroom style of the language is used. The students complain that native speakers talk too fast, or that they don't speak plainly, or that (in the case of spoken English) they use an American (Scotch, Irish, British, Australian, etc.) accent, or that they use too much "slang." The real problem is that students are left to learn as best they can for themselves what the language is really like, and they are misled by well-meaning but underinformed teachers. At the moment they most need help in the form of accurate information and relevant practice, they are on their own.

Supplying realistic oral interpretation, then, is primarily up to the teacher. Text authors ignore it, language conventions disregard it, and school traditions tend to oppose it. Administratively, realistic oral interpretation is easy to avoid, and with impunity. Almost everybody has skirted the issue. The problem is exacerbated by the common attitude that informal language, the level most often employed in real life, is somehow bad. One student teacher we know, who was on a tutoring assignment for a group of foreign students whose interest in natural pronunciation was matched by the desperation of their need, responded to a specific drill on the contracted forms *gonna, gotta, wanna,* etc. by saying almost indignantly, "Oh, I could *never* teach that." For her it was a moral question, and she refused the degrading role of "official linguistic corrupter."

There is one justifiable answer to the question Why ignore realistic pronunciation? The answer is "Because my students don't need it. They have to learn to read, but they will never need the skills of oral communication. They'll never have any occasion to talk to a native speaker." While this is sound reasoning, we feel that in many cases teachers who fail to expose their students to realistic pronunciation are neglecting an important responsibility. In this day of wide-ranging travel, satellite communication, and international cooperation, who can be sure that oral skills in a language may not be useful, indeed necessary? Even in the internationally prominent language of English, difficulty in aural comprehension is reflected in the necessity for specially adapted broadcasts by the United States Information Agency (which not only simplifies the language of various radio programs but also finds it necessary to have announcers pronounce this "easy English" at about 85 percent of normal tempo). A teacher who seeks refuge in the explanation of no need for oral skills should be ready to justify his decision.

The teacher who wishes to adapt his presentation to include realistic oral interpretation—the third side of the contextualization triad—will usually have to supplement his materials. The first step to be taken is an identification of the varieties of language that should be taught. Each variety, or level, should be presented in a context that is consistent and appropriate. Reading stately poetry and engaging in friendly banter require different styles of pronunciation, and the teacher should be prepared for both. However, we wish to reiterate that most oral communication takes place on the informal level. Not many people spend great amounts of time reciting poetry, addressing congresses, or apostrophizing traditional heroes. Even a national president or prime minister speaks informally the bulk of the time. Still, it is desirable to be able to perform at more than one level: this is in fact one of the goals of sound language instruction. Our point is that the cake should be prepared before the frosting is added.

Realistic oral interpretation involves at least three pronunciation phenomena (notably so in English and in varying degrees in all other languages): reduction, assimilation, and contraction. (These are defined, illustrated, and explained in detail in Bowen 1975, pp. 157-174 et passim.) We have observed that there is a formal level of communication which is so generalized in teaching traditions that it needs little specific description. In a general way, we can characterize this level as consisting of lexical items that do not change when they are linked together in sentences. The pedagogy of this speech variety is simply to master the words and learn to string them together in proper grammatical sequences. Other varieties of the language involve changes associated with appropriate levels of usage. This involves the application of sociolinguistics to language pedagogy, to define variant forms and describe the conditions under which they are used.

ILLUSTRATING REDUCTION

Reduction in English involves mainly vowels. There are actually two sets of vowels, which can be called strong and weak, or strong-stressed and weak-stressed, or full and reduced. These two systems can be represented as follows:

Strong

iy I		uw U
ey ɛ	ə	ow oy
æ	ay aw ɑ	ɔ

Weak

iy I	ə	uw
		ow

The strong vowels appear when a syllable has one of the higher stresses, and the weak vowels occur when a syllable is weak-stressed. The difference can be seen in the two pronunciations of words like *convict,* as a noun and as a verb. Note the vowel in the first syllable:

Spelling		Pronunciation	
Noun	*Verb*	*Noun*	*Verb*
convict	convict	kánvìkt	kənvíkt
abstract	abstract	ǽbstrǽkt	əbstrǽkt
conduct	conduct	kándə̀kt	kəndə́kt
project	project	prájè̀kt	prəjékt
produce	produce	prówdùws	prədúws
suspect	suspect	sə́spɛ̀kt	səspɛ́kt

The weak vowel par excellence is /ə/, the schwa, which is the neutral vowel in English. The schwa varies in a large number of particles, or one-syllable non-inflected words in English, with presence or absence of a higher stress. Note how the following prepositions vary in pronunciation as the stress patterns of the sentences they occur in vary:

Context		Pronunciation	
		Full form	*Reduced form*
Full form	*Reduced form*		
Is Casper in?	Yes, he's in the den.	ín	ən
Who's he voting for?	He's voting for Schroeder.	fɔ́r	fər
Where's Schroeder from?	He's from Indiana.	fràm	frəm
Who'd he give the ballot to?	He gave it to Martinez.	tùw	tə
Where's Jensen at?	He's at the laundry.	ǽt	ət
What's it made of?	It's made of steel.	àv	əv

When these prepositions occur finally in a sentence, they are normally pronounced with a full vowel, as they would be if stressed for any other reason (*I said* in *the desk, not* on *it*). But when they occur internally they are typically not stressed, and the predictable result is that the vowels change to schwa.

Forms other than prepositions also follow this pattern. A few examples are:

Context	Pronunciation
I said it and I'm glad.	ət
Eat food that has lots of vitamins.	dhət
What was he talking about?	wəz
There can't be any more jam.	dhər
Where can he be?	kən
Shall we all come early?	shəl
What are his plans now?	ər
June and Alice already came.	ən
Bill or Jack will come later.	ər
Here it seems lonely.	ət

There are some forms that show a greater degree of reduction than just the change of a full vowel to a schwa. In some verb and pronoun forms, certain consonants are dropped.

Full form	Reduced form	Full form	Reduced form
You haven't been there, have you?	What have you done?	hæv	əv
Her father was here yesterday.	I saw her father yesterday.	hər	ər
You saw who? Him?	Yes, I saw him come in.	hɪm	əm
You gave it to who? To them?	Yes, I gave them a new copy.	dhɛm	əm
He came early.	What was he doing?	hiy	iy

The pedagogical problem is compounded by the fact that so *many* of these forms occur in sentences: articles, pronouns, prepositions, relaters, etc. Their very quantity produces a staggering effect on students. How should they be taught? What specifically can a teacher do to help students master the large number of variant forms? We suggest that from the very beginning the variation should be presented to students with at least a rough idea of distribution. For example, *to* is only pronounced /tuw/ when it is cited in a list or for some reason receives higher than weak stress, as when it comes last in a sentence; otherwise—and usually—it is pronounced /tə/. From the first day of class the form /tə/, properly illustrated, should be used and taught. Then of course from that time on, the /tə/ should be consistently used in contexts, styles, levels, and registers where it is appropriate. As often as is pertinent, the descriptive information should be updated so the student knows just what the distribution is, when each form should be used, and where there may be room for choice.

It goes without saying that the teacher himself in his own pronunciation should use the normal distribution of forms such as /tuw~tə/. This sounds self-evident and simple, but it is actually a major stumbling block. Language teachers have carefully trained themselves in the special style of classroom speech. Even if they are willing to change to conversational style when this is appropriate (and lessons should be devised in such a way that it often will be), they may have difficulty and may find it "unnatural" to be natural. Nonnative teachers of a language may have an even greater problem. They may not control the informal levels, having never been taught and in many cases having never developed an awareness of specific variations involved in vowel reductions.

There's the additional problem of professional attitudes. A teacher who is convinced that the reduced forms should be taught may have to work with colleagues who disagree and judge the use of forms like /fər/ in place of /fɔr/ as pernicious.

An example that well illustrates the lack of agreement concerning oral interpretation can be seen in the verb ending which we write *-ing*. Purists and unreconstructed idealists insist it should be pronounced /-ɪng/, but realists know it is usually /-ən/ in informal contexts:

	Pronunciation	
Context	Prestige	Natural
Where are you going?	gówɪng	gówən
Who's he coming with?	kámɪng	kámən
How're you doing these days?	dúwɪng	dúwən

It would be nice if we could simply say /-ɪng/ for formal contexts and /-ən/ for informal. But actually it's not so simple. A study by Fisher (1964, pp. 483-488) points out there are several parameters in the choice of forms: sex (girls use /-ɪng/ more than boys), social class, personality, and mood, in addition to formality. Interestingly, but not surprisingly, certain words are themselves more likely to be more formal or less formal: *interesting* and *correcting* almost always require the /-ɪng/ suffix, while *chewing* and *punching* usually take /-ən/.

So what does the teacher do? The same as before: use both forms, always in appropriate contexts, and explain the distribution as accurately as possible. The deficiencies of the past have been occasioned by ignoring the informal forms— pretending they didn't exist—and leaving the student to struggle on his own when he faces the reality of variant forms. Anticipating the students' needs is certainly a form of adaptation of teaching materials and programs that will improve the overall effectiveness of instruction.

Reduction of vowels, and sometimes of consonants, is the most general phenomenon related to interpretational realism. A second phenomenon, almost exclusively involving consonants (in English), is assimilation.

ILLUSTRATING ASSIMILATION

Assimilation is a process through which pronunciation features of adjacent or nearby sounds change so that the sounds become more similar to each other. A clear example of an assimilation-type modification is the change of the plural ending /-z/ (on a word like *dogs*) which becomes voiceless /-s/ after a voiceless sound (as in *cats*). Another example is the change of the past ending /-d/ (as in *freed*) to /-t/ (as in *passed*). These are well-known changes, and they are more than adequately drilled in typical second-language classes.

Another type of assimilation can be seen in the insertion of "intrusive" consonants to facilitate the transition between sounds that are quite different from each other. An example of this means of adjustment can be seen in the word *dreamt,* pronounced /drɛmpt/. The verb *dream* takes an irregular past tense ending /-t/, which brings /mt/ together. But the transition from voiced bilabial nasal to voiceless alveolar stop seems too much, so a compromise voiceless bilabial stop, a /p/, is inserted between the /m/ and the /t/; as a result, the word *dreamt* rhymes with *tempt.* A similar insertion can be seen in the children's word *thumbkin,* pronounced /thámpkən/, where a /p/ serves as transition between an /m/ and a /k/; as a consequence, the word rhymes with *pumpkin.* Indeed, any word that positions an /m/ before a /t/ or /k/, with a following weak-stressed syllable, will see the introduction of a /p/ as a transition.

Intrusive /p/ is not really a pedagogical problem, because it is relatively rare. But there is a somewhat similar pattern that often causes trouble: the partial assimilation of a nasal consonant to the point of articulation of a following consonant. We say partial, because sometimes the assimilation occurs and sometimes it doesn't. For example, the prefix /ɪn-/ will assimilate (to /ɪm-/) before a /p/ or /b/, but the prefix /ən-/ will not. Thus we get *impact* and *imbed* but *unpacked* and *unbend.* Speakers of other languages learning English are likely to have trouble with one or the other of these patterns, simply because it is rare for a language to show an inconsistent solution where assimilation is concerned.

The assimilation pattern that gives most trouble to learners from other language backgrounds is the palatal assimilation series, strongly characteristic of English, and illustrated by the following examples:

Combined forms	Single item homonym	Pronunciation
Is that *Gus you're* talking about?	gusher	gáshər
Is *Lees your* family name?	leisure	líyzhər
Is *art your* favorite hobby?	archer	árchər
OK, you've *made your* point.	major	méyjər

In these comparisons an alveolar sound combines with a palatal /y/ to form a series of palatal sounds. The pattern is:

$$\left.\begin{matrix} s \\ z \\ t \\ d \end{matrix}\right\} + y = \left\{\begin{matrix} sh \\ zh \\ ch \\ j \end{matrix}\right.$$

This is a pattern of great generality in English, but students unprepared for this type of variation will easily be perplexed. Other languages we are familiar with do not have the same kinds of assimilations; therefore such assimilations are an especially important teaching point in the development of aural comprehension in English. How can the student get practice? We suggest some repetition-integration drills with two parts of a sentence to be combined at the point where assimilation takes place. Note the following:

	Uncontextualized pronunciation	Contextualized pronunciation
I'll really miss / you when you go.	mís / yùw	míshuw
Is this / your only copy?	dhís / yùr	dhíshər
Who's / your sister gonna marry?	húwz / yùr	húwzhər
Has / your father given his consent?	hǽz / yùr	hǽzhər
Why did you beat your brother?	bíyt / yùr	bíychər
Is that / your only chance?	dhǽt / yùr	dhǽchər
When did / you find out?	díd / yùw	díjə
Who'd / you go to see?	húwd / yùw	húwjə

Understanding these variations should help students interpret similar contrasts that are frozen into the structure of the language: for example, where an ending that begins with /y/ has had a palatalizing effect on the final stem consonant. Examples are *race~racial, face~facial, glaze~glazier, moist~moisture, verdant~verdure,* etc.

It would be simple if we could just instruct the student to apply the palatalization rule whenever any of the alveolar sibilants or stops are followed by a /y/ sound. Maybe this is a satisfactory procedure, but we notice there are times when the palatalization doesn't occur or when, to prevent possible misunderstanding, it is specifically blocked. One of our communicants commented, "This suggestion will really aid you," pronouncing *aid you* as /éyjuw/. But then realizing that the sentence could be interpreted *age you* quickly amended the utterance to "I mean it could really aid you" (/éydyùw/). Such pairs where a potential confusion may occur will perhaps keep the contrast alive, even on the level of informal communication:

> Here's the (lease/leash) you asked about.
> The (ruse/rouge) you told me about was no good.
> The (cat/catch) you gave me got lost.

How should this problem be handled in the classroom? The most promising pedagogical approach seems to us to be: (1) use the assimilated pronunciations in appropriate contexts, (2) explain the basic features of the pattern, (3) give students an opportunity to practice the pronunciations—not necessarily to adopt them, though they can if they wish, but to become kinesthetically familiar with them so that when they hear the assimilations used they will have an appropriate interpretation catalogued in their experience.

ILLUSTRATING CONTRACTION

The phenomena of reduction and assimilation occur very frequently in the English language. The third phenomenon, contraction, applies only to specific combinations of words.

We spoke of contractions in Chapter 2, but only in reference to the recognized contractions, those for which a convention in the writing system is available. The convention is the use of the apostrophe to signal omitted sounds: vowels and/or consonants. As we indicated, there are teachers who unfortunately believe these contractions—*he's* for *he is, I'm* for *I am, isn't* for *is not,* etc.—should be avoided in pedagogical materials and perhaps in any written form of English.

This attitude is far stronger with respect to the "unrecognized" contractions that don't have a spelling with an apostrophe. Such forms include *gonna* from *going to, gotta* from *got to, wanna* from *want to, hasta* from *has to, hafta* from *have to, supposta* from *supposed to, usta* from *used to,* and perhaps others. Sentiment for utter condemnation seems very strong among some teachers, and so these common but "suspect" forms have been almost totally excluded from teaching materials. The predictable result is that very few foreign learners of English employ them at any time. Furthermore, many students regard such contractions as corrupted speech and therefore feel they should be excluded from intercultural communication.

Such exclusion can work in the classroom, but when the student is exposed to normal oral communication outside the controlled classroom environment, he is quite often unable to follow the conversation. As he is left by the wayside, he sadly concludes that English is often spoken carelessly and inconsistently.

Why not take him in, let him hear these forms, describe their construction and distribution, let him practice and become familiar with them? A systematic exclusion is certainly a distortion of English as it is used in its natural habitat—by native speakers. Even more important, these forms carry contrastive information necessary to easy communication. Note the following:

How much do you want to teach?	wánt tə	I'd like at least $800 a month.
How much do you wanna teach?	wánə	I am very anxious to get a teaching job.

What do you have to eat?	hǽv tə	The refrigerator's full of food.
What do you hafta eat?	hǽftə	Liver, three times a week.

There are other contrasts like these, and they are not easy for a student to pick up with no assistance.

THE CASE FOR REALISTIC ORAL INTERPRETATION

The effect of reductions, assimilations, and contractions is cumulative. Any one instance alone can probably be interpreted through linguistic redundancy; but when they come in great numbers and combinations, the effect is devastating to the uninitiated. Compare the following two versions of a short sentence in English:

wâchə ɖúwən
hwɑ̀t ɑ̀r yùw dúwɪng

The first has nine sounds in sequence, the second 55 percent more: fourteen. Of the nine, only four or 44 percent appear in the second. So less than 29 percent of the sounds from the formal version are preserved in the informal version. The number of syllables is reduced 20 percent, from five to four. If differences of this magnitude show up in a brief simple sentence, the variation in whole discourses certainly warrants notice in the classroom, especially given the extensive application of informal forms in normal communication.

Teachers reluctant to expand the area of classroom concern to informal styles have several arguments based on: (1) a realization that it would be difficult and would take more classroom time and effort to teach a wider range of style levels (it's hard enough to teach formal English), (2) the belief that students don't really need competence in the use of informal forms, (3) the belief that students can readily learn informal forms later, if and when they are needed, (4) the conviction that misapplication would be greatly more serious if informal forms are used where formal are appropriate than vice versa, (5) the feeling that mixing levels in the same sentence would create serious problems of language etiquette.

They're right; it is more difficult. But they're wrong in assuming that the damage can be repaired later. And it is debatable whether or not misapplied informal speech is a more serious social blunder than misapplied formal speech. Mixing levels is unfortunate, to be sure; utterances like /wə̂təyə gôwɪŋ tùw dúw/ or /hwɑ̀t ɑ̀r yùw gə̂nə dúw/ are anomalies. But the answer is to teach style levels correctly, not to ignore the problems.

The most serious problems concerning interpretational realism deal with attitude: the feeling that certain forms are unworthy of recognition. We feel that if this attitude can be changed, the other problems will diminish and hopefully disappear. It's quite possible that the additional reality would have a favorable effect on the outcome of the language-teaching program, which seriously needs the encouragement of a more successful end product. In brief, *at least a passive comprehension of assimilations and related forms is a must. Production mastery of such forms is advisable and attainable.*

One particular problem is inherent in the responsibility given the teacher. Native English-speaking teachers can rely on their internalized feelings of what the language can do. But nonnatives may not have these feelings, and indeed may have developed a limited range of competence. Explicit materials are needed for such teachers until they can gain familiarity with an adequately wide range of language use. In the meantime they can solicit the help of colleagues, editors of professional journals (through the letters columns), and other professionals. It seems to us obvious that the profession should accept the implications of the cognitivist movement in language teaching and seek to contextualize realistic lessons and materials in realistic settings, with realistic language and oral interpretation.

In Chapters 1 to 3 we have discussed contextualization in three guises: situational, linguistic, and interpretational. Situational realism is easy to comprehend, though not always easy to add to a course if the textbook is deficient. Linguistic realism runs somewhat counter to pedagogical tradition, but can be added to a textbook presentation if the teacher is willing to go beyond the text and produce supplementary dialogs, exercises, etc. Interpretational realism is generally left to the teacher, omitted from textbooks. It is theoretically easy to add, but difficult as a practical matter because of the strong feelings many teachers have against informal patterns and levels. Nevertheless, congruence between the language lesson and the real world is required in all three areas in order to generate communicative, plausible interaction in the new language.

NOTE

1. One of the complications of discussing pronunciation in a written communication is the need to represent sounds by means of writing symbols. This is particularly a problem in English, where the same spelling can represent different sounds, e.g., the *th* of *th*in and *th*en (and *Th*omas and ho*th*ouse), and the same sound can be written several different ways, as the /sh/ sound is in *sh*irt, *s*ugar, i*s*sue, na*ti*on, fa*ci*al, comprehen*si*on, *Ch*icago, mousta*ch*e, and *sch*wa. It is not possible to avoid spellings that stand for sounds, and an organized presentation requires consistency and simplicity. The present chapter is not a presentation of English phonology (see Bowen, 1975, for that), but rather a discussion of a number of issues relevant to teaching oral English. For reference purpose the following symbols are used to refer to the seven English consonants that are ambiguously spelled in traditional English orthography:

Sound and key word	Symbol used in this text	Equivalent symbols used in other texts
*th*in	/th/	θ
*th*en	/dh/	ð, ~~dh~~, ~~d~~, ~~th~~, *th*
*sh*in	/sh/	š, ʃ
a*z*ure	/zh/	ž, ʒ
*ch*in	/ch/	č, c, tš, t ʃ
*j*ig	/j/	ǰ, dž, d ʒ
ki*ng*, si*nk*	/ng/	ŋ

English vowel patterns are described in some detail in the text, but we can at least mention here the pervasive schwa, which is so common in weak-stressed syllables in English, e.g., *a*bout *a* min*u*te *a*go, . . . /əbȃwt ə mínət əgów . . ./. Of seven vowels, four (all weak-stressed) are schwa.

SECTION TWO

USAGE PROBLEMS

CHAPTER 4
LINGUISTIC DEFICIENCIES IN TEXTS

We have observed that the teacher needs to modify his text to suit the background and objectives of his particular class. In addition, we have discussed a variety of ways to contextualize the language being presented. But the teacher also needs to be alert to possible linguistic deficiencies in his text. We realize that at the outset this may seem like an almost impossible expectation. Since many rely on the language textbook as syllabus, reference work, and guide, it might well seem presumptuous for a teacher with limited experience to challenge or tamper with the fundamental grammatical presentation. Fortunately such repair work is not often required, and usually when such problems arise they are as obvious as an omitted line of print on a page. Many are oversights which the author himself would have corrected if they had been called to his attention before the book went to press.

Occasionally mistakes occur in the basic presentation. But far more frequently the error occurs in an exercise or drill in which a hastily written item is simply unidiomatic or wooden sounding. Such errors turn up most frequently in out-of-date texts and those printed in countries where native speakers of the target language may be in short supply. But they sometimes appear in American- and British-produced materials as well. Sometimes the deficiency consists of an incomplete or sketchy introduction to the new material; some texts fail to allow adequate opportunity for assimilation. Such deficiencies are not technically linguistic errors, but simply presentations that lack synthesis or opportunity for the student to digest the new material. Other presentations lack clarity. In this chapter we will examine ways of coping with these problems.

DEFECTS IN EXERCISES

Certainly the most easily detected and simply corrected linguistic errors are those that occur in language exercises. Since there is a higher probability of error here than elsewhere in the lesson material, the teacher should always edit the exercises carefully by doing every item himself before using them in class or assigning them as homework. Students can simply be told, without elaboration, which items to omit; or they can be given a corrected version of a drill sentence. If the work is being done in class, the teacher, as a "partner" of the textbook author, can briefly solicit from his students ways in which the occasional defective sentence can be improved (or if suggestions are not forthcoming just offer them himself).

You will recall an exercise discussed in an earlier chapter. Which statement seems to you unidiomatic?

1. Mr. Adams had a nice flight.
2. The Wilsons had a wonderful trip.
3. Marilyn had a good time at the dance.
4. The secretaries had a grand vacation.
5. Jim and you had an exciting Fair.

The obvious difficulty comes in item 5. We do not use *have* in reference to someone's simply *attending* an event, although we can use it in reference to someone's *hosting* an event: *They had an exciting party last night at their place.* (It is improbable that *Jim and you* hosted a fair.) In addition, it is somewhat curious and unlikely to inform someone that he had an exciting time. If sentence 5 is not simply omitted, it could be revised in one of several ways:

Jim and Ann had an exciting time at the fair.
I heard that you and Jim had an exciting time at the fair.

You and Jim had an exciting party. (I really enjoyed myself.)

I heard that you and Jim attended an exciting fair.

The second and fourth revisions employ more difficult sentence structure than the original, and the last item departs from the *have* verb which is being reviewed. The third example is close to the original syntax, but it introduces a new use of *have*. In addition, we see that *Fair* has also been written in lower case in all the revisions. Noting these several complications, we can see why it is often simpler to omit an unsatisfactory item than it is to perform major surgery on the original. It would even be advisable to work out a simple system with students to delete faulty items by drawing a line through them. This would help facilitate review.

Once in a while an entire exercise strikes one as contrived and unidiomatic. With reference to the key that follows this exercise, select the response that is noticeably wrong.

1. What are used for living in?
2. What are used for wearing?
3. What are used for putting books on?
4. What are used for sleeping on?

Key: 1. Houses are.
         2. Clothes are.
         3. Bookcases are.
         4. Beds are.

One would expect *shelves* (or *tables, desks,* etc.) to be the appropriate response to item 3. Americans and British alike put books *in* bookcases. We showed this exercise (from a recent text acquisition) to a colleague formerly with the British Council; he confirmed our feelings about this drill. He noted that the book mentioned in the exercise would have to be on top of the bookcase—probably in horizontal position. Also, item 4 might well be *sleeping in*. He also indicated that the entire exercise consisted of "language instruction questions" not representative of actual speech. In the event the exercise were retained, one might omit item 3. Or we might recast the sentence in any of the following ways:

Acceptable responses

What do you put books on?	Shelves *or* On shelves.
What do we put books in?	Bookcases *or* In bookcases.
Where do we put books?	In bookcases.
What's used to put books in?	A bookcase *or even* Bookcases *or* Bookcases are.

In short, we would allow any contextually acceptable and grammatically correct response; and the other sentences would be responded to in the same fashion. The third revision requires the student to furnish the preposition himself, and it could generate answers such as *In libraries* and *In bookcovers* if the student had sufficient vocabulary. These sample revisions involve suggestions not only on how to deal with the *in/on* confusion but also on how to make the questions in the exercise sound more conversational.

When examining the language of exercises, we should recognize that there are sometimes national (regional) differences not only in pronunciation but also in lexicon, spelling, and syntax. Thus *Frank is in hospital* and *Have you a new tyre?* should be recognized as fully correct British English sentences that may be more familiar to many of our students than the American versions: *Frank is in the hospital* and *Do you have (Have you got) a new tire?*

The occasional Alice-in-Wonderland language of exercises is sometimes the result of an author's stretching the language to fit some rule, real or imagined. For instance, subject-verb concord requires that "two or more singular subjects joined by *or* or *nor* take a singular verb, agreeing in person with the nearer subject." This rule results in virtually unheard of exercise items such as *Either she or I* am *going*. Native speakers avoid this construction (see Evans and Evans 1957, p. 23) with

Either she's going or I am.   *or*
One of us is going.

Similarly, the rule requiring objective case for objects of prepositions can lead to such nonsense as *Whom were you speaking to?* Even in formal settings, *To whom were you speaking?* is preferred over the preceding. And in the broad area of informal spoken and informal written English, *Who were you speaking to?* is expected and appropriate (see Mittins et al. 1970, p. 107). The teacher should be on guard against exercise items which do not reflect normal spoken and written usage. The related problems of grammatical Old Wives Tales and divided usage are prevalent enough that we will devote a substantial portion of the next chapter to them.

DEFECTS IN BASIC PRESENTATIONS

Clear-cut Errors

Less frequent and less obvious than the distorted language of some exercises are the language errors that now and then crop up in actual presentations and reviews. One illustration is a preposition review that appeared in a recent text. A legitimate item was

Did they have the *privilege of* hearing him perform?

But juxtaposed with this was the sentence

Did they *object to* his traveling abroad?

Here the author inadvertently mixes two quite different grammatical constructions: the preposition governed by a previous word (a noun in the example) and the two-word verb (or verb plus particle attachment).

The teacher could either eliminate the inappropriate *object to* sentence, or capitalize on the situation to contrast two-word verbs with prepositions. It would also be possible to present a paraphrasing exercise:

They (liked/favored) his   They *approved of* his
   going to college.   going to college.
They (disliked/rejected the   They *objected to* his
   idea of) his marrying   marrying Anna.
   Anna.

The teacher would then return to the preposition review, which was the central matter being presented.

Incomplete Presentations

In addition to clear-cut errors in language presentations, there are defects stemming from *incomplete* presentations. Just as the teacher can confuse the student by an uncertain gesture (The teacher says, *What's that?* in reference to a piece of paper on a table, and the student might suppose he is referring to a book on the table, the table top, or the entire table), so the textbook author can blur distinctions that are inherent in the language, and thereby misinform the student.

For example, a recent textbook presented alternate future forms so that students might express future ideas with *be* plus *going to* as well as with *will*:

> *Directions*: Here are two ways to express the future:
> I will climb that mountain.
> I am going to climb that mountain.
> Your teacher will say a sentence in which there is a verb expressing future action. Repeat the sentence, but use another verb form to express the same future act.
> 1. I am going to tell you a secret.
> 2. Helen Simpson will get married.
> 3. She is going to marry a boy from Montreal.
> 4. They will live in Canada.
> 5. They are going to leave by plane next week.

It is useful, of course, for the student to learn alternate ways to express future time; and the author provides here some welcome continuity among sentences. However, in substituting one form for the other as freely as he does, the author gives the faulty impression that these two forms are simply interchangeable. But native speakers do not freely substitute one for the other in all situations.

Students of English will naturally wonder what differences there are between the various ways of referring to future time. The problem can be aggravated by textbook presentations that ask for one pattern as a substitute for another, without an explanation of the difference in meaning or at least a contextualization that reveals that difference. Let's look at some of the problems.

The traditional verb form called "future tense" is the modal construction with *will*. Also in common awareness is the so-called periphrastic future with *going to*. These two forms contrast in meaning, but the difference is often not clear, a situation made more difficult by a conspicuous overlap in meaning. The basic difference is that *will* as a modal implies the exercise of volition, the act of choosing and promising, whereas *going to* involves a simple prediction based on the observation of a known fact or intention. The difference can be seen very clearly in a sentence pair with second-person pronoun forms, where personal desire versus intention is expressed:

> Will you have some more ham? (May I offer you more?)
> Are you going to have some more ham? (Do you intend to have more?)
> Will you help Joan tomorrow? (a request)
> Are you going to help Joan tomorrow? (an inquiry)

It is likewise usually apparent in sentences with first-person pronouns:

> I'll help Mary with her math assignment. (I am willing to assist her.)
> I'm going to help Mary with her math assignment. (My present plan is to assist her.)

Note that the first sentence can readily take a continuing *if*-clause, *if she wants me to*. The second sentence suggests that Mary has already been consulted or indeed that she has already asked for my assistance. Reference is to the future culmination of a present intention.

The contrast is not always so clear in third-person sentences. Note the following:

> It will rain tomorrow morning.
> It's going to rain tomorrow morning.

Am I in a condition to promise a rain? Perhaps with *will* I can express my strong confidence that it will rain, whereas with *going to* I merely express my expectation. But this is a comparison of degree of confidence in a prediction more than a genuine difference in meaning.

Other pairs in third person, especially in questions and negative sentences, reveal a difference:

Who'll bring sandwiches? (Who is willing to offer?)
Who's going to bring sandwiches? (Who has offered?)
John won't visit Uganda. (He's unwilling to go there.)
John's not going to visit Uganda. (His itinerary doesn't include that country.)

Sentences expressing a condition, which if fulfilled amount to a promise, take *will*:

If you visit Mexico City, you'll be surprised at the cool temperature.
If you ask her, she'll do it.

Such sentences almost never appear with *going to*. Sometimes the condition can be implicit:

Take that bus; it'll get you to the university.
This map will show you how to get to Edinburgh.

The implication is that *if* you take that bus, *if* you use this map, the result will follow.

If a personal intention is expressed, not as a promise, but as a planned action, *going to* is used:

He's going to stay home tonight and study.
Next week I'm going to buy a new bike.
She's going to have a baby.
Help! It's going to drop!

Will cannot be substituted in these sentences without a considerable change in meaning.

As if *will* and *going to* were not enough complexity, there are several other ways to express subsequence (or futurity) in English. There are several lexical expressions that imply future, such as *plan to, expect to, hope to*, etc.; and even more difficult to sort out are the use of regular simple present forms, continuous present forms, and the verb *be* with *to*. The latter indicates a future course of action imposed from a source beyond the concerned persons:

I'm to introduce the speaker tonight. (It has been decided
   by someone that I will make the introduction.)
The Chinese are to take care of building the railroad.
   (The plan gives them this responsibility.)

This is almost equivalent to *supposed to*:

I'm supposed to introduce the speaker.
The Chinese are supposed to build the railroad.

It should probably be noted that strictly speaking there is
no grammatical category of future in English—no "future
tense." English verbs are inflected for past or nonpast; future,
or more specifically "subsequence," is expressed by the special
forms cited above. But any nonpast form is compatible with
the expression of futurity, and regular present forms of the
verb (simple or continuous) can be used for this purpose.
When this happens, the futurity must be specified by external
modification, that is, by the presence of an adverb (or adverb
phrase or clause) that definitely indicates future time. Note:

I leave tomorrow at 9:00 a.m.
He arrives at midnight.

The implication is that these plans are fixed by circumstance;
the person concerned has little or nothing to say about it; he is
controlled by a train schedule or by orders from above.
   An event that can be controlled by planning is expressed by
the present continuous. Note the following:

I cook steak tonight. (a planned event over which I have
   no control—I'm just the cook and I do what I'm told.)
I'm cooking steak tonight. (an event I have planned and
   arranged)

Compared to these, *I'm going to cook steak tonight* also refers
to a planned event, specifically the expected result of my
present intention.
   On the other hand, a sentence which implies a promise
cannot be expressed by *going to* or by a simple or continuous
present verb form: *I'll know Arabic next year* but not #*I'm*

  #   This symbol is used to signify the use of faulty grammar or other
       common non-English.

going to know Arabic next year or *#I know Arabic next year* or *#I'm speaking Arabic by next year.* This is an event which can be arranged only by our own volition or will.

The simple present or continuous present verb form cannot be used to describe events that cannot be controlled or planned:

#It rains tomorrow.
#It is raining tomorrow.

But we can express an expectation (*It's going to rain tomorrow*) or even a promise, if we are sufficiently skilled in meteorology (*It will rain tomorrow; I'm sure*).

It should be clear from these examples that the expression of subsequence in English is not a simple matter. But this is no reason to gloss over the facts and simply not attempt to describe the distribution, or to merely teach the forms and leave the students to figure out when to use them. The student who says to his teacher "Am I going to hand in my assignment next Wednesday?" needs more help than to be told there are alternate ways of expressing the future in English.

Since *will* and *be going to* are generally not interchangeable, it would be best to avoid a simple "tense" substitution drill. Instead of replacing one form with the other, one could concentrate on the new form—*going to.* A simple exercise would consist of students' using this phrase, merely providing the necessary inflections and agreement between the subject and the accompanying verb *be.* It could be alternated with *be -ing-*verbs, as in this revised version:

Directions: Fill in the blanks with the appropriate form. Use contractions where these are appropriate.

1. Guess what! Helen Simpson _____ *going to* quit her job today.

2. Why? _____ she *going to* get married?

3. Yes. She _____ *marrying* a boy from Montreal in a few weeks, and

4. they _____ *going to* live in Canada.

5. In fact, they _____ *flying* up there right after the wedding.

(*Note*: *Going to* could have been used in all of these sentences, but for the sake of variety another form is used. What is it?)

In brief, it would be advisable to present the two forms—*will* and *be going to*—independently so that each can become firmly established. Then they can be contrasted to show how the latter is used to express intention (*I'm going to pick him up at 10:00*) or certainty (*It's going to rain tomrrow*) and the former, willingness (*Ok, I'll help him*), future facts (*The postman will be here soon*), and conditions (*I'll be there if I can*). In order to cope with rare textbook deficiencies such as these in language presentations, the teacher may need to consult a reference work. For example, those interested in this specific contrast (*will* and *be + going to*) could see C. E. Eckersley and J. M. Eckersley (1960, pp. 165-167), Marcella Frank (1972, pp. 75-77), or Eugene J. Hall (1974, vol. 2, pp. 188-190).

Another limitation of the *will/going to* presentation is the seemingly insignificant matter of not indicating when contractions should be used. When material is uniformly presented in *un*contracted form, the student is often led to believe that contractions are somehow unnecessary or even substandard, and therefore inappropriate. This can lead to a minor but permanent handicap notably in the oral production of pronouns and auxiliary verbs.

Besides learning that the pronoun is contracted with the verb (*He's going*), students should be aware that in speech, noun subjects tend also to be combined with auxiliary verbs, even when they are separated in writing: Thus *Jack will be along soon* becomes *Jack'll be along soon* when spoken, unless the speaker is striving for a particular emphasis or preciseness.

Those who learn the *un*contracted form initially often find it almost impossible to use contracted forms later on. Their feeling that contractions are slurred, lazy shortcuts to communication is sometimes reinforced by teachers with strong feelings about language etiquette but limited awareness of actual language usage. Textbooks which ignore the matter of when to contract and when not to contract subjects, verbs, and negatives are deficient in this respect. The conscientious teacher will need to compensate for this by redesigning the presentation as illustrated earlier in this chapter; or with a more advanced class he could underscore earlier work with contracted forms by considering those special occasions when *uncontracted* forms are called for. He might even devise an activity such as the following:

Directions: In spoken English, we normally contract the pronoun subject with the following verb; or we contract the verb with *not*. Look at the following exceptions and be prepared to tell why they are not contracted:

	Explanation
1. Is Frank here yet? Yes, *he is.*	(Contractions of subject and verb not possible at the end of a sentence.)
2. He's always late for his appointments. He is not always late. This is the first time he's been late all year.	(Contradiction suggests avoidance of contraction.)
3. You sound annoyed. I am annoyed. You've been critical of everyone who's come in here today.	(Contraction avoided in order to provide emphasis.)
4. I guess I have been rather critical. Yes, it's not like you. You're usually very patient.	(Emphasis during this affirmation transformation again tends toward uncontracted form.)

Students: Notice now the *contracted* forms in the sentences above. Which verbs in addition to *be* are contracted?

For discussion: Are the responses in items 2 and 3 normally appropriate if one is speaking to his employer or teacher? Are there alternative ways of expressing negative ideas like these with people we respect?

There is at least one further consideration for teachers using exercises of the *be going to* variety in a class where the objective is to develop fluent, natural-sounding speech, and that is when to contract. Notice in the following examples that *be going to* (like *will*) serves as a future marker for the verb that follows.

Take that bus. It'*ll* (get) you to the university.
Next week I'*m going to* (buy) a new bike.
Later this year she'*s going to* (go) to Europe. (Later this year she'*s going* to Europe.)

In the final item, we see that when the main verb (or infinitive) is *go,* we may use *go* in the present continuous form. This construction illustrates a significant contrast in pronunciation. As we have noted in Chapter 3, many teachers are reluctant to acknowledge usage facts in this situation: for example, that the *going to* future marker reduces to *gonna*. But no such assimilation is possible when *going* is a main verb followed by preposition *to*. Thus we have:

She's *going to* the hospital because . . . (going to)   /gowɪŋ tə/
She's *going to* have a baby.   (gonna)   /gənə/

It would be a simple matter to prepare a supplementary exercise to provide practice with this contrast:

Directions: In this mixed practice, say the sentence aloud. Use *gonna* where possible.
1. She's *going to* the Health Center this afternoon.
2. Later she's *going to* study in the library.
3. I might see her at the Health Center because I'm *going too.*
4. Are you *going to* have an eye examination?
5. Yes. Then I'm *going to* work at the chemistry lab after that.

(For ready-made exercises see Rutherford 1968, p. 22, or Bowen 1975, pp. 164-170.)

What can we conclude from our discussion of the presentation on *will* and *be going to*? First, oversimplification can be dangerous. In this instance, both structures are future forms, but they are not freely interchangeable. The teacher must edit or alter the presentation in order that his students not acquire basic misconceptions. Second, atypical or unidiomatic presentations of the language need to be avoided. In our example, appropriate contractions and assimilations must be incorporated, not as an alternate form but as the standard form for conversation and oral reading of printed material. Also, there are refinements in oral applications of the language that the teacher must expect to attend to. But of course the object of the teacher should be to make only essential modifications.

Faulty Sequence

Sometimes the fundamental sequencing of materials in a text may not suit the teacher. The highly controlled audio-lingual sequence proceeding from *be* and the simple present or present progressive on through the perfect tenses, modals, and conditional may seem stultifying. A visiting master teacher from Eastern Europe indicated recently that it was not uncommon in her country for an entire year to be spent on a single tense before students were introduced to another one. Occasional contemporary texts retain a strictly grammatical focus, plodding through interminable transformations— embedding, nominalizing, passivising, etc. At the other extreme is the text which essentially ignores any grammatical sequence. "Communication" or "situation" is king; but teachers and students alike are often troubled by the seemingly spotty, random introduction of language items.

In neither case is it recommended that the teacher attempt to overhaul the sequence or structure of the textbook. Earlier chapters in this book suggest a variety of ways in which new life can be breathed into the often mechanical exercises of the rigidly sequenced language text. Two antidotes have proven helpful for those using modern texts that seem to be aimless as far as specific language items are concerned. One is to prepare supplementary exercises in areas where students demonstrate a particular need. Another is to develop a lexical-grammatical-situational checklist (or series of short achievement tests) to demonstrate concretely what progress has been made and what is expected. Yet another, though perhaps obvious, suggestion is for the teacher to familiarize himself with the objectives and methodology recommended by the author.

While wholesale resequencing is not recommended, occasional adjustments may be necessary. For example, the teacher may use a learning strategy that requires his students to ask for clarification when something is not understood. If the author happens to have deferred useful *wh*-questions for a few lessons, the teacher can simply introduce this question form earlier as needed. One text used in Miami, where street names are often numbers, failed to introduce numbers until rather late in the course. This proved to be a genuine limitation for mature students who needed such information. Obviously, a teacher using this text would need to introduce the numbers earlier. Likewise, in the teaching of reading and writing, key linguistic features must be introduced before the student is required to cope with them: for example, the use of quotation marks and related punctuation as well as conventions for reporting speech should be introduced before students are required to write pieces utilizing conversation.

THE NEED FOR INTERNALIZING

The present decade has provided us with important insights regarding language acquisition. We perceive, for instance, the active role the learner plays in the language learning process. We realize it is not remotely possible for him to be "taught" the language by his simply memorizing the various combinations of structures that can be combined to make up the sentences of the target language; instead, he must grasp the much more finite set of rules which generate language discourse. But as every experienced language teacher knows, the student must have the opportunity to assimilate his new insights and develop proficiency in employing them. Early in our "cognitive" era Dwight Bolinger (1968) pointed out that

> "teaching" something involves more than the initial grasp of a rule. That may of course be taught by a deductive presentation. But being given a rule is like being

introduced to a stranger; we may be able to recognize him on later encounters, but cannot be said to know him. Teaching a rule involves not just the phase of grasping but the phase of familiarizing. To imagine that drills are to be displaced by rulegiving is to imagine that digestion can be displaced by swallowing. [P. 34.]

In brief, the teacher needs to enable the student to digest the language and internalize it. Even drill should provide a meaningful experience.

In those classes where there is inadequate assimilation of the language, the fault often stems from the teacher's failure to utilize his textbook properly; he may skip blithely along, breezing through chapter after chapter without really attempting to learn how well his students can employ what they have been exposed to. But sometimes the fault lies with the materials being used. Some textbook presentations and exercises are so mechanical and so exclusively grammar-oriented that students find it difficult to see the relevance of the activities they are engaged in. The foregoing chapters on contextualization are designed in part to provide relevance and thereby an important means by which students can assimilate what they are being taught.

Synthesis

In addition to providing context and situation, the teacher can complement the text by utilizing insights and employing techniques which contribute to assimilation of the language. An example of this is synthesis.

English methodologist J. N. Hook, for instance, refers to high school texts with thirty-five to forty pages devoted to the use of the comma. While contemporary texts are becoming much more succinct, it is not unusual to find two dozen segments or more on when to use and when to avoid using the comma. Hook (1965, pp. 329-332; 1972, pp. 393-398) strongly recommends helping students to master such detail by inductively examining related samples of items and then extracting a few important organizing principles under which the several uses can be grouped. "The heart of the plan," says Hook, "is a reduction in the number of comma rules." He then provides examples and illustrations on how the many rules for the use of commas can be reduced to as few as three: (1) preventing possible misreading, (2) setting off nonessential elements, and (3) separating words or word groups that are similar in form and function. He suggests that if one's text discusses thirty comma rules,

> instead of having the students learn the thirty rules, let them see that all thirty are simply subdivisions of the three basic principles. Teach the thirty as specific illustrations and insist only that the students understand thoroughly the big three. [1972, p. 397.]

Particularization

Assimilation of language concepts can be aided not only through synthesis but also through particularization, or breaking the material down into more digestible bite-sized chunks.

A few contemporary language texts resemble reference works more than they do instructional materials for building lessons in the classroom. One such book covers six dozen uses of modals in a single review lesson. Another widely used book for second-language learners introduces an amazing total of five dozen two-word verbs in fewer than three pages, plus illustrating multiple meanings for some expressions and demonstrating that certain two-word verbs are separable while others are nonseparable; then at the end of the lesson there are between 250 and 300 supplementary two-word verbs and dozens of compounds. Still another book introduces six future verb forms in a single lesson. While these prominent texts illustrate extremes, there are numerous books that contain occasional overloaded lessons.

One way to cope with lesson overload is to spend considerably more time on that lesson. Also, construction of supplementary exercises may be necessary; or parts of some lessons can be introduced gradually. In the case of the highly compact two-word verb lesson, a handful of such expressions could be introduced each week throughout the term or school year. Many, if not most, could be grouped situationally and then analyzed for structure:

> *lying down* or *turning in* for the night
> *dozing off*
> *waking up*
> *getting up*

> *taking off* and *hanging up* one's pajamas
> *putting on* one's clothes

> *sitting down* to eat
> *finishing off* the cereal
> *getting up*
> *cleaning off* the table
> *washing up* the dishes
> *setting off* for work

Another sequence might involve social exchanges:

> *look up* a number in the telephone directory
> *pick up* the receiver
> *call up* a friend

talk over the events of the day
be asked to *come over* (or *drop over*) for a visit
hang up the receiver
put on a jacket
go out the door and *start off* for the bus stop
get on a bus
get off at the campus
drop by the dormitory

Let us next consider how the ineffective presentation on modals might be improved. The overloaded presentations on modals contained rules and short examples, followed by notes on syntax and finally by exercises involving paraphrase and deduction. This is the way the modal *must* was presented:

The modal auxiliary must:
1. Deduction about present situation.
   She isn't happy. She *must* be lonesome.
2. Deduction about present action.
   They're running to class. They *must* be late.
3. Deduction about future: the need for *going to.*
   He's picking up his books. He *must* be *going to* leave.
4. *Must* with the meaning of necessity; present moment.
   She simply *must* see me this instant!
5. *Must* with the meaning of necessity; future moment.
   You *must* return the book in two weeks.
6. No past form for must; past necessity uses *had to.*
   They *had to* get a physical examination.
7. *Must* as a general truth; no adverbial of time.
   Man *must* satisfy his basic wants.
8. *Must* used in negative: this means it is imperative that something not be done (not that it isn't necessary to perform some act).
   You *mustn't* laugh at him when he stutters.
9. Absence of necessity: *not* plus *have to.*
   You do*n't have to* take the final examination.

A similar set of illustrated rules was presented in the same lesson for all of the other modals as well. This staggering catalogue almost bewilders the native speaker, let alone a second-language learner. In addition, the explanations were expressed in rather difficult language ("continuative aspect," "past hypothetical result," "volition," "synonymous with," "a past opportunity which was exploited," "conjecture," "an obligation of the past not discharged," "advisability," "inevitability," etc.); moreover, a rather large corpus of grammatical terminology was used.

Our suggested adaptation restricts the focus not only to the one modal auxiliary *must* but to a particular use of *must*. Besides this effort to space and particularize the presentation, we attempt to aid student assimilation through synthesis: We have collapsed the first three rules into one. Finally, difficult terminology is eliminated, and supplementary examples are provided. Here, then, are three possible ways of treating the *deduction* meaning of the modal auxiliary *must*:

Alternative One:

Explanation: Often we see something happening, and we try to guess or figure out the reason for it. For instance, we see some students at 9:05 in the morning running into a school, and knowing that school starts at 9:00 we decide they are late for school. We can express this by saying, "They must be late." *Must* indicates our statement is a conclusion that we have figured out for ourselves.

Additional examples:

Situation	Your conclusion
He's picking up his books.	He must be going to leave.
Her fiance is still out of town.	She must be lonesome.
There are puddles of water in the road.	It must have rained last night.

Alternative Two:

Explanation: Often we experience something and we try to guess or figure out the reason for it. There are different ways to express deductions like this.

(a) We often use *may* or *might* when we have only a small or uncertain clue—as in the following example:

It may be raining outside.
Why do you say that?
I think I heard it thunder a moment ago.

(b)   When we are quite certain, we use words such as *probably* with our verb; or we use *must.*

It's *probably* cold outside. I just saw some people come in with overcoats on.
It *must* have rained last night. There are some puddles of water in the road.

(c)   When the evidence is very strong, we omit *probably* or *must,* and simply state our conclusion.

It rained last night. Look, there are puddles of water everywhere.

Alternative Three (A situational/inductive presentation):
Conversation practice 1:
Mr. Cohen: Look at those boys run.
Mr. Sanders: Yes. Now they're turning in at the school.

Mr. Cohen: They must be late for class.
Mr. Sanders: Yes, they very probably are.

Conversation practice 2:
Isn't that Dr. Murphy?
Yes. He's really speeding.
Oh oh, he turned in to the hospital.
There must be an emergency.

Grammatical note for exercise: *Must* and *probably* in situations such as this express our deduction—conclusions we arrive at from the evidence available to us.

It should be kept in mind that the above adaptation on the use of the modal has been restricted to *explication* only, and to simply one meaning of *must*. We have not sampled the many available exercises, drills, and class activities for practicing this form. And naturally there are still other ways to provide explication. For example, Marianne Celce-Murcia (crediting T. R. Hofmann with the insight) identifies two broad categories of modal usage—situational and logical: requests for permission falling into the first category; deductions into the second.

Of the many possible modal exercises, we might mention the following: (1) reading selections and dialogs incorporating modals; (2) paraphrase exercises (completion or multiple-choice) in which nonmodal sentences are converted to modal usage; (3) data requiring comment (news report: 20 percent chance of rain tomorrow / *It could rain tomorrow*; 95 percent chance of rain tomorrow / *It will very likely rain tomorrow*; (4) cloze-type narrative requiring modal completion; (5) modal or conditional statement with multiple-choice paraphrases—the student identifying which paraphrases are correct, which are false, and which there is too little information to make a decision on (there can be more than one multiple-choice answer that is true or false, or no true items, for example).

Practice

We have seen a variety of ways the teacher can assist his students to assimilate new language material: not skimming through one's text too quickly, contextualizing the language, synthesizing when possible (as with the comma rules), and particularizing by spacing out complex instruction and concentrating on one application at a time.

Still one more means of furthering assimilation is to provide adequate exposure and practice. This is important whether one accepts the older views of overlearning, memorizing, and habit formation or contemporary views of cognition, rule learning, and socially appropriate communicative application. To repeat Bolinger, "Teaching something involves more than the initial grasp of a rule" (p. 39). Probably the most deadly form of exposure is monotonous repetition of mechanical drills. A variety of means compatible with student/teacher temperament should be incorporated, keeping in mind Stevick's (1959) "technemes" of class activity (pp. 45-51) and McIntosh's (1974) timely caution against chaos in the name of motivation and variety (p. 83). Varied practice can range from oral and written exercises to writing, field trips, role play, competition, interviews and reports, plays, songs, inquiry sessions, films, tapes, language laboratories, community assignments, debate and panels, class exchanges, individual study, and paired activity. The emphasis, as Paulston suggests, should be on meaningful and communicative responses rather than on rote practice, and certainly the varied activities employed should provide carefully planned language practice, avoiding oppressive teacher dominance and aimless activities-for-activity's-sake.

THE NEED TO CLARIFY

Presently, more so than for several decades, meaning is recognized as important to the language teacher. It isn't enough that the student drill until responses become automatic; he must also understand what he is saying, so that he can use the language appropriately. For example, the teacher would do well to incorporate meaningful explanations of grammatical forms whenever possible. More often than necessary, the student is expected to acquire the new form through osmosis or memorization.

One particular area of difficulty is the preposition. Beginning with *on the table* and *in the drawer*, it is not difficult to extrapolate to *on the floor* and *in the box*, or *on the wall* and *in his pocket*. Little effort is needed (students can arrive at sound conclusions themselves) to determine why one is said to hold even a rather large ball *in his hand* (the fingers slightly encompassing it), or why one is told to place an *X in the circle on the blackboard.* Similarly (for intermediate students) cows may be said to be *in the pasture* but coyotes live *on the prairie* (the former being fenced). Even political boundaries influence our speech so that we're *in Kentucky* but *on the ocean.* The idea of being covered or surrounded compels us to say *He's swimming* in *the river today, but he was boating* on *the river yesterday.* When someone's taking a nap on a Sunday afternoon, *He's resting* on *the couch in the family room,* but once under the covers, *He's in bed.*

Logical explanations can also be made for *on/in* contrasts when used with various modes of transportation. Here the guidelines are simple: The first rule is that we use *on* with a means of transportation which in no sense can contain a passenger: bicycle, horse, roller skates, balsa raft, barge, etc. If

a vehicle can contain or surround a passenger, we apply the second rule, which specifies *mobility.* A vehicle where mobility is possible and normal will usually take the reference *on*: bus, train, airliner, ship. In these cases the passenger is perceived relative to a surface. But where mobility is restricted, the reference will usually be made with *in*: car, taxi, limousine, small plane, buggy. This is true even if the "containing" vehicle only partially encloses the passenger:

canoe, rowboat, liferaft, convertible automobile. With *in* it is felt that the passenger is positioned with respect to the enclosing sides of the container. Thus *in* is occasionally used with reference to a large vehicle where mobility is possible if the meaning is specifically *enclosed in*—in contrast to being on the outside. For example, "Do you think he's very cold out there?" "Oh, no. By now he's already in that warm bus."

The preposition *by* is another matter entirely; it can be used in reference to either group of conveyances: *by* car, *by* ship, *by* train, *by* mule.

Another area that baffles most foreign students studying English is the use of articles. Students are often provided with only perfunctory information such as which indefinite article to use before words beginning with a vowel (*a* before *peach* but *an* before *apple*). The remaining uses are to be learned simply through extensive exposure to the language. Incomplete presentations like this can be supplemented over a period of time by illustrating how articles function with plurals, with mass and count nouns, with initial and subsequent references to a noun:

I saw *a* horse and a mule yesterday. *The* horse. . . .

with objects that are individual or which we consider to be unique within a particular frame of reference:

Tom went to *the* door.
Please bring in *the* newspaper.
When did man first land on *the* moon?

and occasionally with generic reference:

The giraffe has a long neck.

It is quite appropriate to provide assistance of this kind in order to speed up the acquisition of a language.

In other areas as well, logical explanations can complement practice and exposure to rules. While it is sound pedagogy to minimize the terminology used in instruction, such perennial problems as *Food* is costing *too much here* can be dealt with effectively by distinguishing between active (dynamic) and stative verbs. (For example see Quirk and Greenbaum 1973, pp. 46-47.) When functioning in the verb phrase of the sentence, the latter, of course, do not take the progressive form. Likewise, confusion about when to use the simple past and when to use the present perfect can be reduced by providing insights into the "aspect" of these verbs. In addition to the implication of recency that is often suggested in the present perfect, this tense shows the relevance of the past action to a present condition. Consider

	Tense
He *lost* his wallet (yesterday).	past
He *has lost* his wallet.	present perfect

The former focuses on a *past incident,* while the latter focuses on a *present condition,* namely his being without funds. The present perfect tense basically expresses the relevance of an action to the present moment. One interpretation of relevance is recency—an event from the near past, often continuing right up to the present. But recency is not a necessary interpretation, since events from a more distant past can be relevant to the present (e.g., *I have been to Madrid only once, and that was in 1940*). Notice in the two example sentences that follow how the past tense dissociates the event mentioned from the present, even to the extent of implying that the person referred to is no longer living, while the second sentence leaves open the possibility that the situation reported can be changed.

	Tense
I never *heard* Winston Churchill speak.	past
I*'ve* never *heard* Britain's Prime Minister speak.	present perfect

The teacher of a linguistically homogeneous group of students is in a unique position to clarify instruction, by adapting appropriate presentations to accommodate specific differences between the students' first and second languages. Difficulty occurs, for instance, when one word in the native language is the equivalent of two or more words in the second language. This is sometimes referred to as a lexical split. It can be illustrated by *hacer* in Spanish, which is sometimes expressed in English as *do*, sometimes as *make*, and sometimes by other expressions (Hagerty and Bowen 1973, pp. 1-71). Let us assume a class of native Spanish speakers. The teacher would first present the areas of rather direct equivalence. Then she would gradually introduce areas of divergence.

In treating the areas of equivalence for speakers of Spanish who are studying English, she would stress the pro-verb characteristics of *do* (*I like classical music and Frank likes classical music* → *I like classical music and Frank* does *too*). She would also alert her students to the fact that 40 percent of the time *hacer* is equivalent to an English expression other than *do* or *make*. As she moved into areas of divergence, she would stress the use of *do* functioning as a tense carrier—and thus avoid errors such as:

#Did he changed the money?
#Does she wants the book?
#But he *did* came to the party!

And she would introduce the various ways in which *do* and *make* combine with particles to form two-word verbs (*He* made up *with his girl friend*). (See Hagerty and Bowen, pp. 37-38.)

This short discussion of ways to clarify grammar instruction is not intended to suggest that language be presented through elaborate grammatical explanations. Such an approach is usually doomed from the start. It *is* suggested, however, that calling attention to the system, regularity, or logic of a construction can greatly benefit the student in initial stages of language acquisition. This can be handled briefly, and for less advanced students it can be conducted in the vernacular. As in the *hacer/do-make* illustration, it is possible—and generally very desirable—to handle grammatical clarification indirectly, through exercises and language activities that focus on the point at hand.

In Chapter 4, we have considered various ways of coping with linguistic deficiencies in language textbooks in order to provide students with sound instruction in usage. These range from editing or correcting unidiomatic drill exercises to supplementing anemic language lessons. We have also seen how the teacher can complement the textbook by synthesizing complex rules or focusing on smaller units of instruction during a given presentation. Such modifications, we feel, promote easier and more rapid assimilation of language—as do the occasional explanations of grammar recommended in the final section of the chapter. In brief, we have learned how to evaluate language presentations and improve upon those that are deficient. The following chapter complements this one by presenting data on contemporary usage so that we might be better attuned as to what to teach.

CHAPTER 5

PROBLEMS IN CONTEMPORARY USAGE

When it comes to problems in usage, the language teacher needs to be on the alert for unidiomatic exercise items or defective presentations comparable to those illustrated in Chapter 4. And he also needs to be aware of usage conventions that might be touched on in the course of class discussion or writing assignments. This is particularly true when using contemporary textbooks that are not heavily structured grammatically and texts that have a situational or communicative-competence orientation. Such books open the door to constructions and expressions that would have been postponed or completely avoided just a few years ago. The purpose of the present chapter is to survey areas of usage that today's teachers may need to cope with when using such books. The three areas of usage to be dealt with here are "Old Wives Tales," items of divided usage, and anomalies in the language.

OLD WIVES TALES

Old Wives Tales consist of usage "rules" which have somehow been passed down to this generation but which in fact do not represent actual spoken or written conventions. Their promulgation constitutes a kind of linguistic quackery, which has about as much use in language teaching as magical amulets or talismans do in medicine or horoscopes and astrology do in the modern science of astronomy.

Fortunately, they seldom occur in contemporary texts. But the fact that they appear at all, coupled with the substantial number of laymen and rather surprising number of teachers who give some credence to them seems to warrant their inclusion in the present discussion. Generally speaking, however, the usage matters discussed in this section can be thought of as complementary to one's text. Only occasionally will a teacher be called on to remedy a textbook presentation that includes an Old Wives Tale.

For the purpose of illustration, however, we will examine one of these persistent falsehoods which is often taught by well-meaning teachers even to native speakers. The following was taken almost verbatim from an early English-as-a-second-language text:

Substitution Drill (Tense Replacement): *shall/will* distinction; review of tenses—simple form

Directions: Change the verbs in the following sentences to *past* and *future* tenses.

1. I come here every day.
   (*Examples*: a. I *came* here yesterday.
                 b. I *shall come* here tomorrow.)
2. He *speaks* Spanish well.
3. She *pays* little attention to her professor.
4. John *sleeps* late every morning.
5. We *eat* lunch in a cafe.

Appendix: Sample conjugations (Verb: *To study*—simple form)

Future tense

I shall study	we shall study
you will study	you will study
he will study	they will study

That the *shall/will* distinction is simply not observed in contemporary English is almost a cliché in most modern English texts. Indeed, there is considerable doubt that the usage described was ever current. Yet very recently one English-as-a-second-language book written by native speakers appeared with the declaration that one of the two uses of *shall* was to express future time in the first person, but "only in formal writing." As most are aware, the generally circulated *shall/will* rule stipulated that in expressions of simple future, *shall* was to be used in the first person, *will* in the second and third persons. But in expressing determination, *will* was to be used in the first person and *shall* in the second and third persons. The rule has been traced back to seventeenth century grammarians (George Mason 1622 and Johannis Wallis 1653) who articulated it initially, and to eighteenth century schoolbook grammarians (William Ward 1765, and Lindley Murray 1795) who elaborated it into dizzying complexity.

Condensing the voluminous writing on this subject, we find that the grammarian-concocted *shall/will* rule had an impact on the English-speaking world—greater, however, in England than in America. Emancipation from the artificial constraint came earlier in the United States. Close to half a century ago, Leonard's usage study in America found two-thirds to three-fourths of the judges approving sentences in which *will* replaced *shall*. A more dramatic piece of evidence surfaced from a 1930 Bell Telephone survey of conversation between American adults: a grammatical analysis of the language used in 1,900 telephone conversations, totaling 79,390 words. *Will* as an auxiliary was used 1,305 times in 402 conversations, whereas *shall* as an auxiliary was used just 6 times in 6 conversations (Pooley 1974, pp. 47-52, and Mittins et al. 1970, pp. 97-102).

By 1949, Lewis found that only 10 percent of his 468 respondents insisted on the *shall/will* distinction. De Boer et al. in 1951 and Pooley in 1960 and 1974 indicated that teachers should not differentiate between *shall* and *will*. From England in 1970, a survey of 55 troublesome usages revealed that the sentence *I* will *be twenty-one tomorrow* was one of only eleven sentences with majority approval for use in both speaking and writing (Mittins, pp. 13 and 102; see also Pooley, p. 209).

In brief, the substitution drill cited earlier attempts to teach a usage distinction which is not made by the vast majority of educated native speakers of English, not even in formal written English.

If some form of this exercise is retained, the teacher can point out that *will* (or in informal speech *'ll*) is now used to express a future or later action. Teachers should be aware that occasionally an attempt has been made to justify the "*shall* rule" by claiming that *'ll* is the contracted form of either *will* or *shall*. The fallacy of this assertion can be demonstrated by citing tag-question forms—e.g., *He'll come, won't he?* (never *shan't he*). In fact, *shall* demonstrates its advisory function by taking a unique short-answer form:

Shall we go?
    Yes, let's.

While the use of *shall* as a future marker is not per se wrong, it is nevertheless so uncommon that it is best avoided. At another time, students will learn that *shall* is used mainly for certain advisory questions such as *Shall we go now?* or *Shall I tell him you're here?* And on other occasions students will be introduced to additional future expressions such as *be going to*. It may be of interest to *teachers* to know the *shall/will* rule, but there is no point at all in teaching it to students.

The drill presented earlier could be adapted as follows:

Response Exercise: Past and Future Review

Directions to teacher: This is a response exercise in which your students will review the meaning of certain present-tense statements regarding habits and customary actions, at the same time reviewing past and future forms. You can either read the basic sentences yourself or have better students say them as naturally as possible. Two students will respond to each statement; they can be selected individually by a gesture from the teacher at the moment the answer is due. Encourage variety in the adverbials of time. *Will* (or more informally the contracted form *'ll*) is to be used uniformly for future ideas. In summary, a number of matters will be reviewed in this activity simultaneously:
- present-tense forms used to express habits and customary actions
- irregular past-tense forms

- the future time form using *will* (normally *'ll*)
- adverbial expressions of time
- proper intonation for statements
- proper selection of personal pronoun in responses

In addition, students will receive controlled practice in responding to statements, by rephrasing or interpreting them.

1. *Speaker A*:   I come here every day.
   Speaker B: Oh. Then you came here yesterday.
   Speaker C: And you'll come here tomorrow.
   (*Yesterday* can be replaced with *Wednesday* or *last month*, etc. *Tomorrow* can be replaced with *next week*, *Sunday*, etc.)
2. *Speaker A*:   I walk (or jog) a mile every morning.
   Speaker B:
   Speaker C:
3. *Speaker A*:   I watch the 11:00 news on television.
   Speaker B:
   Speaker C:
4. *Speaker A*:   John sleeps late every morning.
   Speaker B:
   Speaker C:
5. *Speaker A*:   We always eat lunch in the same cafe.
   Speaker B:
   Speaker C:

Leaving *shall* and *will*, we turn to another pair of verbs— *can* and *may*—which have been something of a bugaboo in English usage. The grammar book rule said that only *may* could be used for permission-seeking and granting. *Can* supposedly was to be limited to an expression of ability. Evans and Evans feel we leave "the realm of language" and enter the "intricacies of politeness" in broaching the *can/may* question; Quirk and Greenbaum, Frank, and the Eckersleys see the choice as one of greater or lesser formality. At any rate, the Leonard survey, reported in 1932, found that over 75 percent of the linguists approved the sentence *Can I be excused from this class?* as "standard, cultivated colloquial English." The Bell Telephone study of 1930 disclosed that *can* was used 396 times and *can't* 228 times (a total of 624) in contrast with 60 uses of *may* and no uses of *mayn't* (Evans and Evans 1957, p. 81; Quirk and Greenbaum 1973, p. 52; Frank 1972, p. 97; Eckersley and Eckersley 1960, p. 197; Pooley, pp. 131-133). Of course since informality is a factor, we might well expect *can* to predominate in the usually informal telephone situation. *May* predominates in formal written English, but consider Evans and Evans' comment on the negative: "In refusing permission, *you may not* is felt to be disagreeably personal and dictatorial and *you cannot* is almost universally preferred (p. 81). Again the Old Wives Tale prohibition obscures the facts of contemporary usage. Sentences such as *Can she go with us?* are not merely permissible but actually preferred in usual speaking situations.

Still another Old Wives Tale is what Pooley refers to as "the much taught but erroneous rule that 'a sentence must not end with a preposition.' " The Eckersleys refer to the

> superstition among some English people that a sentence must not end with a preposition. They think it is more "correct" to say:
> "*At* what are you looking?" than:
> "What are you looking *at*?"
> ... this "rule" is broken by every English-speaking person and has been ignored by almost every English writer within the last seven centuries. . . . There is a story that Winston Churchill, furious at having some end prepositions in a paper that he had written "corrected" by an overzealous secretary, sent it back with the corrections marked in red and a note: "This is the sort of English *up with which I will not put.*" [Pp. 281-282. Also see Pooley, p. 4, and Quirk and Greenbaum, p. 144.]

Pooley indicates the "rule" was created by writers who had been trained in Latin grammar and who desired to "transfer some of its elegance to English." Since "Latin did not permit the placing of a prepositional element at the end of a sentence, someone drew up the 'rule' forbidding this structure in English" (p. 4). While this structure is not common in formal English (perhaps as a concession to the prestige of supposedly educated usage), prepositions at the end of sentences have "every right to be there on the grounds of custom and the idiom of the language." Moreover, says Pooley, "the absurdity of the rule is emphasized by an amusing inversion of it: 'A preposition is a bad thing to end a sentence with!' " (p. 4).

And half-informed people are also concerned about what we *begin* a sentence with. Some hold to the superstition that it is somehow improper to start a sentence with a coordinator such as *and* or *but* as in the last sentence. But such words are really quite acceptable since they provide needed coherence without the heavy effect of adverbial conjunctions such as *however, moreover,* etc. Evans and Evans indicate that coordinating conjunctions like *and, or* and *but* can

> be used to show a relation between independent sentences. Actually, this is only a question of punctuation, of where we put a period and a capital letter. A sentence which begins with a coordinating conjunction could have been printed as a continuation of the preceding sentence. In current English we like short sentences, and a long sentence is sometimes easier to read if it is printed as two independent sentences. [Pp. 113-114.]

The problem with some grammatical Old Wives Tales is inflexibility and overgeneralization. Take, for instance, the rule requiring use of the objective case for the object of the preposition. The net intended to scoop up infractions such as *Between you and I, she drinks heavily* (one of the most rejected usages in the England survey; Mittins et al. 1970, p. 11) also hauls in *Who was she talking to?* While the most formal levels do permit the well-starched *To whom was she talking?*, the *Who . . . to* combination is a *must* in all other situations. Mittins, for example, found that 68 percent of somewhat severe respondents accepted the sentence *Who was he looking for?* in the three categories of informal and formal speech and informal writing, some saying they would even use it in formal writing (pp. 105-107). A rather ludicrous usage occurs when those who recognize that ending a sentence with a preposition is a fact of life nevertheless insist on retaining the objective case: *Whom was she talking to?* Evans and Evans explain that the interrogative *who* is an "invariable form" like

© 1971 United Features Syndicate, Inc.

what and *which*; they point out that English differs from Latin in *not* requiring the objective form for interrogatives that appear as the object of verbs or prepositions. They note that "sentences such as *whom are you looking for?* and *whom do you mean?* are unnatural English and have been for at least five hundred years." They add that *To whom did you speak* is unnatural word order. People follow the *whom* rule to their own disadvantage; they claim: "To most of their countrymen, the unnatural *whom's* sound priggish and pretentious" (p. 556).

Another problem in case arises through an inflexible insistence on the nominative case following a linking or copulative verb. Strict adherence to the rule produces *It's I*—an impossible locution. Leonard's 1932 survey showed that even the uncontracted *It is me* was established at that time. And the sentence *I suppose that's him*, which was in the disputable category when Leonard conducted his study, was in the "established" category thirty years later. The *Dictionary of Current American Usage* reports that "in natural, wellbred

English, *me* and not *I* is the form of the pronoun used after any verb, even the verb *to be* (Evans and Evans, p. 294; see also Pooley, p. 67; Quirk and Greenbaum, p. 103).

Still another Old Wives Tale is the proscription against the use of *like* as a conjunction, *as* being considered as the only proper form. The matter came to a head amusingly during this past decade when a few prescriptivists objected to a cigarette commercial—on the grounds not of health but of improper language use. "Winstons taste good *like* a cigarette should" was supposedly "bad grammar." The tobacco company capitalized on the publicity and retaliated with the slogan, "What do you want—good grammar or good taste?" Frank refers to this advertisement and to the sentence *He looks* like *he needs more sleep* in illustrating how "*like* may occur as an informal alternative for the conjunction *as . . . .*" She adds that "although condemned by some, this use of *like* as a conjunction is common even among educated speakers (p. 267). *Like* as a conjunction appears in the writings of Shakespeare, More, Sidney, Dryden, Smollett, Burns, Southey, Coleridge, Keats, Shelley, Darwin, Newman, Bronte, Thackeray, Morris, Kipling, Shaw, Well, Masefield, and Maugham. Evans and Evans agree:

> There is no doubt but that *like* is accepted as a conjunction in the United States today and that there is excellent literary tradition for this. There is no reason why anyone should take the trouble to learn when *like* is a conjunction and when it is a preposition. [Pp. 276-277.]

Another usage issue that is still aired on both sides of the Atlantic is the split infinitive. Leonard said it was "both a discovery and an aversion of nineteenth-century grammarians." His survey found it to be established usage. A 1970 survey in England (Mittins et al., pp. 71-72) disclosed a 66 percent acceptance in informal speech (though only 19 percent acceptance in formal writing). Eckersley and Eckersley shed the following light on this usage:

> Some grammarians condemn the use of the 'split infinitive' . . . , e.g. 'to quickly agree,' 'to really understand.' But the split infinitive dates back to the thirteenth

century and can be found in the work of many famous authors.

Fowler says: 'A split infinitive, though not desirable in itself, is preferable to either of two things, to real ambiguity or to patent artificiality.' [P. 235.]

The *Dictionary of Contemporary American Usage* charges that "the notion that it is a grammatical mistake to place a word between *to* and the simple form of a verb . . . is responsible for a great deal of bad writing by people who are trying to write well." The "rule" on split infinitives, it is held, "contradicts the principles of English grammar and the practice of our best writers." Avoiding the split infinitive often means dropping the infinitive construction entirely, and this "may lead to wordy paraphrases that are not good English" (Evans and Evans, pp. 469-470). In summary, the much maligned split infinitive is quite acceptable on the informal level, but because of the tender sensitivities of some, it is advisable, when convenient, not to split the infinitive—as in this sentence. The error in the Old Wives Tale is not that this construction should always be used, but rather in proclaiming that the split should never be used.

One final Old Wives Tale will help to illustrate two things: first, that such rules are not limited to syntax; and second, that language teachers in particular need to keep abreast of changes in usage. The old rule insists that plural foreign borrowings (*data, strata, stamina*—Latin; and *phenomena, criteria*—Greek) be used with plural verbs. But Mittins points out that the predominance of the *-s* plural in English as well as the occurrence of singular nouns ending in *-a* (*replica, diphtheria, euthanasia*) not surprisingly results in the *"data"* group "occasionally, often, or regularly" being construed as singular. In his 1970 usage survey in Great Britain, Mittins used the sentence "The data *is* sufficient for our purpose." It was fifth from the top in acceptability: 82 percent in informal speech and 55 percent in formal writing (pp. 30-32). Pooley calls our attention to a dramatic shift in attitude toward this word during the past three decades. The Leonard survey in 1932 rated *The data* is *often inaccurate* as illiterate; the 1971

Crisp survey rated it as "established." Its acceptance is reflected in A. S. Hornby's classic dictionary for foreign students: in the 1974 edition of the *Oxford Advanced Learner's Dictionary of Current English, data* is described as usually having a singular verb; and the sample sentence *The data is ready for processing* is cited. According to Pooley, "The plural form of a foreign word is determined solely by its use in English" (pp. 59-60).

Obviously the teacher must be wary of Old Wives Tales and be sensitive to the realities of current language use, most particularly to the reaction that the claimed correctness or the actual usage will generate in any specific social group.

USAGE CHANGES

An experienced overseas teacher recently confided in us that she and her colleagues were guilty of quibbling with intermediate and advanced students over debatable items of usage. As she observed, valuable time is often wasted on hair-splitting issues that can confuse more than enlighten the students. The purpose of this section on divided usage is to call attention to a cross-section of usages which at one time or another have been considered faulty or nonstandard but which are now generally accepted on one or more usage levels. The levels we refer to are informal speaking, formal speaking, informal writing, and formal writing. Legitimate changes from past usage suggest that this process is active and that more changes can be expected in the future. During the transition from one preferred form to another, it is obvious that at any given time a newly accepted usage might be approved by only a slim majority of one national group. In his reference work on usage, Pooley identifies speech forms that would suitably be covered on elementary, early secondary, and upper secondary school levels; and significantly he identifies those items which would best be deferred or not taught at all. For the senior high school teacher he illustrates eight usage items no longer considered nonstandard English. Similarly, this section of the chapter might well serve as a guide to the kinds of usage items that we no longer need to spend much energy in eradicating. Of course such decisions need to take into consideration the level of our instruction (beginning, intermediate, advanced) and also the kind of proficiency we're trying to develop. In the past many teachers considered it their task to instruct students in the conventions of formal usage; today the goal is far more frequently to acquaint students with appropriate informal spoken and written English. Teachers of some advanced courses may desire to acquaint students with both informal and formal usage conventions. Whatever the goal, the teacher who is familiar with current usage facts can adapt his text more easily and use his class time more economically.

For convenience in teacher reference, we will refer primarily to three sources: Pooley, Evans and Evans (Americans), and Mittins et al. (British). In order to provide a broader scope, we will restrict our comments on each item; the teacher who is interested can consult the references for further details.

Verbs

Some grammarians have objected to the word *and* plus an infinitive following verbs such as *go, come,* and *try. Come and see me* has been considered nonstandard; *Come to see me,* standard. Pooley (pp. 124-125) indicates that both expressions are acceptable; he quotes the *Oxford English Dictionary* among his sources. Evans and Evans indicate that *try and* is standard English in both England and America for *try to,* though used somewhat more frequently in Great Britain (p. 524). Mittins' Great Britain survey showed majority acceptance only on the informal spoken level (p. 51).

Formerly the only correct past tense form of *dive* was considered to be *dived.* (One of our teachers used to insist that "a dove [dowv] is a bird of peace.") Pooley cites 1927 and 1932 surveys which showed *dove* to be considered illiterate in England and divided usage in America, but from that time *dove* began to gain currency in both countries. The 1971 Crisp survey showed *dove* to be established; Pooley indicates that *dove* is now used more than *dived,* which is slightly more formal (pp. 134-135). Evans and Evans indicate that either form is acceptable in America but not in Great Britain (p. 139).

The subjunctive *if he were* has been contrasted in grammar books with *if he was* (unreal condition or wishing)—the latter being labeled substandard. Pooley indicates the former is normally used in writing and cultivated speech but that the latter "may be considered standard English." Use of *was* is more "a question of taste than of 'correctness' " (p. 56). Evans and Evans indicate that *was* has been used in literary English as past subjunctive for over three centuries and is still the preferred form. *Were* is preferred in the *If I were you* sentence but in *if he were/was given a chance, was* is more common (p. 547). Mittins' survey used the sentence *They would accept this if it* was *offered,* and the rating for informal speech was very high—77 percent, but low—21 percent—for formal writing (p. 75).

Have got has been strongly objected to in sentences such as *I've got a book,* grammarians arguing that *I have a book* was the only acceptable form. Pooley shows *have got* to be acceptable. The Leonard survey (1932) rated the sentence *I have got my own opinion on that* as "standard, cultivated colloquial English" (pp. 144-145). Evans and Evans indicate that *have got* has been used in literary English for over four hundred years in sentences such as *We've got plenty of time,* or *He's got an apple in his hand* (p. 201). Both Pooley and the Evanses agree that *gotten* is an appropriate past participle in sentences such as *I've just gotten a splinter in my hand.* The Mittins survey ranked the sentence *We have got to finish the job* very high (84 percent) in informal speech but very low (16 percent) in formal writing (p. 35).

Proven as the past participle of *prove* has been labeled "archaic," "Scottish," or nonstandard. But Pooley marshals a number of authorities to show that it is "accredited and acceptable," having been used widely by reputable writers in both the nineteenth and twentieth centuries and being "extremely common in speech" (pp. 156-158). (Interestingly, one of our recently edited manuscripts—an essay for a language text—was returned by the editor with *proved* crossed out and *proven* written in.) Evans and Evans describe *proven* as "respectable literary English," used in America more often than *proved*, but in Great Britain less often than *proved* (p. 399).

Aggravate has been considered a substandard version of *exasperate*. Pooley refers to various sources, including the early Leonard survey, which rated *That boy's mischievous behavior aggravates me* as disputable, and the recent Crisp survey, which rated it established (pp. 122-123). Evans and Evans indicate that *aggravate* meaning *annoy* is a colloquialism, "not used in formal speech or writing" (p. 21).

Teachers have long been annoyed with students' using *infer* for *imply* as in *Their success, his attitude inferred, was due to his own efforts.* Evans and Evans concede that such substitution has taken place for several centuries and is used so commonly today that many authorities recognize it as an equivalent expression; the Evanses recommend, however, that careful writers maintain the original distinction (p. 326). Mittins indicated the *infer* substitution had not achieved majority acceptance. But the survey disclosed that 68 percent of the students surveyed approved it in informal speech in contrast with only a 17 percent approval by examiners; in formal writing 51 percent of the students approved it as compared with 6 percent of the examiners who were surveyed (pp. 68-69).

The use of *loan* as a verb is "condemned in Great Britain" say Evans and Evans, even though it is a "very respectable verb" which has been used for nearly eight hundred years. "It is thoroughly acceptable in the United States. . ." (p. 281). In the United States, the past tense of *lend* (*lent*) is seldom used in speech or writing. The preference is for *loaned,* the past tense of *loan.* But Mittins reports that the sentence *They will loan you the glasses* received a very low rating, even students giving it only 27 percent acceptance (p. 104).

Turning to subject-verb concord, we will look first at the situation where two singular subjects are joined by *or* or *nor.*

According to the traditional rule, the verb in these circumstances must always be singular. Pooley defends the use of the plural verb in the sentence *Frank or Jim* have *come on alternate weeks to my at-homes.* He accepts Margaret Bryant's position regarding current usage: "In informal and in spoken English, a plural verb is sometimes used when the substantives joined [with *or* or *nor*] are singular" (pp. 77-78). Evans and Evans indicate that in such a sentence as *Either he or I (am) responsible,* some would prefer *is,* some *are,* but most would recast the sentence and avoid the awkward sounding construction (p. 23). In Great Britain the sentence "Neither author nor publisher are subject to censorship" did not receive majority approval even in informal speech— although students did muster a majority rating in this one category (p. 80).

Pooley catalogues a number of situations involving subject-verb agreement where the traditional rules cannot be strictly applied (p. 209):

My old friend and advisor *is* sick.
There *is* wealth and glory for the man who will do this.
The entire list of candidates *were* interviewed.
The kind of apples you mean *are* large and sour.
The captain as well as most of his men *were* never seen again.
He is one of those boys who is . . .

Pooley charges that textbook rules have been too inflexible and have failed to pinpoint the underlying principle that "the verb always agrees with the *intent* of the subject regardless of its form" (pp. 73-82). Evans and Evans take a parallel view, approving such sentences as

Neither Dorothy nor Andy are at home.
The sheriff with all his men were at the door.
One half of the population are illiterate.
Not one of them were listening.
A pile of books were on the table.

and even a possible plural verb with a plural-form title such as *The Canterbury Tales* (Evans and Evans, p. 22):

> *The Canterbury Tales* are required reading in this course
> and so is Hamlet.

Americans, however, would never use this customary British
sentence:

> Australia are winners in the tournament.

Nouns and Pronouns

While the possessive case with inanimate nouns occurs as early
as Beowulf, it has been rejected in more recent times on the
grounds of logic (inanimate things cannot "possess"). Pooley
acknowledges that the *of* phrase has generally replaced the *-s*
genitive, but defends the acceptability of the latter, especially
in phrases such as *the house's roof, the clock's hands*, etc.
Evans and Evans (like Quirk and Greenbaum) provide a very
elaborate explanation of the genitive and genitive categories.
The Pooley example, called a descriptive genitive, is not
considered an error. But this form, they say, tends to be
avoided by using when possible an uninflected *clock hands* or
hands of the clock if the descriptive word (or genitive) is to be
emphasized (pp. 197-198).

Virtually until the present time school children have been
harangued about the need to use the possessive before the
gerund (*I didn't approve of Frank's saying that*), since
theoretically the uninflected noun or objective pronoun (*him
saying that*) suggests a dislike of Frank rather than of his
actions. This is one of the eight usage items that Pooley
recommends be dropped from high school English instruction.
In 1932, language specialists involved in the Leonard study
approved the sentence *What was the reason for Bennett
making that disturbance?* although the group as a whole rated
it as disputable usage. But by 1971 it was rated "established"
in the Crisp survey. Pooley also defends as perfectly acceptable
"a building whose windows were broken" (pp. 111, 168-169).
Evans and Evans acknowledge that some grammarians find the
objective case offensive here but that the majority of people
now use it this way; the objective case before the gerund is

therefore "acceptable contemporary English" (pp. 245-256). In the British Isles the sentence *What are the chances of* them *being found out?* was approved for informal speech by 81 percent of the students and even 51 percent of the examiners; but only 27 percent of the students and 3 percent of the examiners approved it for formal writing (p. 67).

When a pupil does poor work, it *is not always the fault of the teacher.* This sentence has been criticized because the pronoun has no specific antecedent. Pooley points out that altering it would result in awkwardness. He says that "though grammatically anomalous, this construction is both useful and prevalent" (p. 117). (Of course *it* as a "prop" word or expletive is not challenged in sentences such as *It's going to rain* or *It seems odd.*) Like *it*, the pronoun *this* has also been required in English books to have a specific antecedent. Evans and Evans, however, contrast the use of *this* with *that*: "The word *this* is preferred when the reference is less specific. It is often used as a summarizing word and means 'all that has just been said' " (p. 510). Consider also the contemporary informal *this* in *This guy came up and . . .*

Another schoolbook rule is that *each other* may be used in reference to two people but that *one another* is required for more than two. The old Leonard survey, says Pooley, labeled the following sentence as standard: *The members of that family often laugh at each other*; he concludes that there is "no justification whatever" for the rule (pp. 138-139). Evans and Evans hold that *each other* and *one another* have the same meanings and are interchangeable (pp. 148-149). In Great Britain an almost identical sentence to that above received high approval (84 percent) for informal speech but only 36 percent approval for formal writing (p. 33).

The use of *myself* in place of *me* has also been castigated in the textbooks. But Pooley quotes many sources in its defense, saying that it is useful in that it is less blunt and more impersonal than *I* or *me*; "it is felt to be modest, polite, and courteous." He argues that from the standpoints of literary authority, current usage, and psychological need, its use in such sentences as *I gave a folder to all present, not omitting* myself is totally acceptable (pp. 154-155). Evans and Evans take a slightly conservative view, acknowledging that it can be used in absolute constructions, and after linking verbs and as part of a compound object. But they see it as old-fashioned when used as subject (p. 310). Mittins recalls that Leonard's survey, taken in America over thirty years ago, found 62 percent of those surveyed in approval of a sentence such as *They invited my friends and myself.* He reports a more conservative attitude in England, with just 50 percent approving it for informal speech, and a general acceptability rate of only 33 percent over the four categories (p. 64).

Rule books have been quite clear in classifying as singular, the indefinite pronouns such as *everyone, everybody, anyone, anybody, neither,* and *either*—requiring not only a singular verb but also a singular subsequent pronoun reference. Pooley acknowledges that the singular is predominant (particularly in America) but feels that the rule is too inflexible. He notes that both the 1932 and 1971 usage surveys rated the following sentence as "established": *Everyone was here, but they all went home early.* However, the sentence *Everybody bought their own ticket* was rated by both as "disputable" (pp. 83-85). Evans and Evans take a similar position. The indefinite pronouns are normally singular, they say, though *neither* and *none* normally require a plural verb; some of the other indefinite pronouns may occasionally take a plural verb. They cite *Everyone was here but they have left* and *If anyone calls tell them I have gone* as standard English. "The best modern writers," they conclude, "like the great writers of the past, sometimes use the singular *he* and sometimes the plural *they,* depending upon the circumstances rather than on any rule of thumb about the 'number' of an indefinite pronoun" (p. 240). Mittins reports that the sentence *Everyone has their offdays* was approved by a substantial 72 percent for informal speech but only 19 percent for writing (p. 103). Mittins also indicates that the sentence *These sort of plays need first-class acting* was submitted to the 457 member panel of judges. The speaking-writing differentiation was great: 53 percent approved it for informal speech but only 33 percent accepted it for *in*formal writing (p. 85).

Modifiers

The words *farther* and *further* have caused some confusion. Some textbook writers indicate the former should be restricted to space and the latter to degree. But Pooley indicates the two can be used "interchangeably in all meanings but that of *in addition*, or *more*, in which *further* is approved." The expression *all the farther* he says is very common but not acceptable in formal spoken or written English (pp. 142-143). Evans and Evans, on the other hand, indicate that *farther, farthest* can apply only to distance; *further, furthest* can be used in reference to distance as well as to mean *additional* (p. 172).

The use of what many feel are only adjectives (*loud, soft, quick, slow*) in an adverbial position is offensive to many teachers. Pooley prefers to think of "two-form" adverbs (*loud/loudly, soft/softly*). When to use each depends on the situation. He holds that the *-ly* group predominates in declarative sentences while the other group predominates in imperative sentences. The *-ly* form is also required, he says, at the beginning of a sentence, and between parts of a verb phrase (*he had quickly thrown*) (p. 58). Pooley also accepts *real, sure,* and *awfully* in informal situations, noting that *real* is less informal than *sure* as an adverb (pp. 159, 127). Evans and Evans deal with these words individually but in essence agree with Pooley. Regarding *loud,* for example, they indicate that "this word is as truly an adverb as it is an adjective," and they include a quotation from Spenser using *loud*. Evans and Evans feel that *sure* as an adverb offends too many people to warrant its use except in *sure enough*. They do accept *real* as an adverb, however (pp. 384, 491, 410). In England, the sentence *That's a dangerous curve; you'd better go slow* averaged 54 percent acceptance in informal speech and writing combined. Curiously, 67 percent of the examiners approved it but only 52 percent of the students and a mere 46 percent of the teachers (p. 108).

The position of the adverb *only* has worried purists for years, but Pooley argues that fear of ambiguity is unnecessary, for in sentences such as *I only had five dollars* there is no misunderstanding. He adds that stress and not position decides the meaning (pp. 87-88). Evans and Evans concur, indicating that when *only* is placed between the subject and the verb it is not construed to modify only the verb or the subject (pp. 337-338). In England the test sentence was *He only had one chapter to finish.* (Note the possible ambiguity in this sentence—a stress on *chapter* providing one meaning, and a stress on *finish* providing another.) Says Mittins:

> ... the "spread" between the extremes of Informal Speech and Formal Writing was very wide (79 per cent), but the speech/writing differential was none the less as usual overshadowed by the informal/formal distinction. Acceptability in Formal Speech (29 per cent) was not much more than half that (54 per cent) in Informal Writing. [Pp. 61-62.]

Turning to dangling constructions, Pooley feels that, like split infinitives, some are quite harmless, as in the sentence *Considering our costs, the price is low.* Texts covering this usage item, he says, should provide realistic examples of when one can and when one cannot omit a subject following an introductory participial or gerund phrase (p. 106). Pooley then quotes Evans and Evans who charge that "the rule against the 'dangling participle' is pernicious and no one who takes it as inviolable can write good English." They show that many participles are used independently much of the time and that often an unattached participle is "meant to apply indefinitely to everyone, as in *facing north there is a large mountain on the right. . .*" (pp. 354-355). The acceptance of dangling constructions in England is not clear since a different type of sentence was presented the panel there than those Pooley and the Evanses were discussing. In the Mittins' survey the sentence was *Pulling the trigger, the gun went off unexpectedly.* The average acceptance was understandably low: 17 percent (p. 88).

Pretty as an adverbial intensifier such as *very* is recognized by Evans and Evans. They do not suggest its level of acceptance (p. 391). The sentence *The instruments were pretty reliable* was ranked in England as follows: 84 percent tolerance for informal speech; 51 percent, informal writing; 15 percent, formal speech; and 7 percent formal writing—thus producing the widest spread of any usage (p. 48).

One final adverbial is the use of *literally* to mean *figuratively* but as a kind of intensifier. Evans and Evans explain that "When, for example, on a hot day someone says *I'm literally melting,* he means *I am figuratively melting* and the meaning

of *figuratively* here is 'not literally' " (Evans and Evans, p. 280). When the panel in England rated the sentence *His eyes were* literally *standing out of his head,* 79 percent of the students, 62 percent of the noneducationists, but only 28 percent of the examiners approved this for informal speech; it was understandably rejected by all groups in the area of formal writing (Mittins et al., p. 63).

Debatable adjective usage often occurs when using comparatives and superlatives. One of these is the *as . . . as* construction following a negative verb. Evans and Evans point out that some grammarians demand *so . . . as* in a sentence like *He is not as serene as his mother;* however, they say this is not necessary and that "most good writers and speakers" prefer the *as . . . as* construction (p. 42). The Mittins survey corroborates this stand. The sentence *He did not do* as *well as the experts had expected* rated the highest acceptance of all the items surveyed: 95 percent for both informal situations and 67 percent for formal writing (p. 25).

The sentence *He could write as well or better than most people* involves the dropping of *as* in the comparison *as well as.* Evans and Evans say that some object to these kinds of telescoping, "but they are acceptable, and customary English." He illustrates a rewriting (*He could write as well as most people, or better*) if one wants to please the grammarian (p. 107). Mittins reports 64 percent acceptance for informal speech but rejection in other applications (p. 89).

Some texts continue to require *different from* instead of *different than.* This is one of the usages that Pooley advises English teachers to stop teaching (p. 209). Evans and Evans agree, pointing out the eighteenth century genesis of the rule and the impressive catalog of good writers using *different than.* While *different from* is acceptable, there are absolutely no grounds for rejecting *different than* (p. 136).

Pooley challenges the inflexible requirement that the comparative and never the superlative be used in comparing two persons or things. He shows that the superlative is often used "not only in colloquial speech where it is quite common, but in the published work of careful writers" (p. 113). Evans and Evans bear this out with an impressive list of prominent writers who do not follow the rule. The "rule," he claims, is an imaginary one:

> In Latin the comparative form is used in a comparison involving two things and the superlative is a comparison involving more than two. Some grammarians claim that this ought to be the rule in English too, but the practice of our best writers does not bear them out. [P. 106.]

Pooley is equally critical of those who claim it is not possible to modify or compare such "absolute" adjectives as *dead, square, round, equal, unique,* and *circular.* Comparison *is* logical, he contends, in the sense that we are considering "degrees of approach to something perfect, dead, or unique." He contends that a "rule" which ignores accepted practice in early and modern literature, conclusions of prominent linguists, and language practices of educated people "becomes futile and ridiculous" (pp. 114-115). Also rejecting both the logic and soundness of this rule, Evans and Evans say:

> Attacks on grammatical constructions made in the name of logic are usually bad logic. And they are always bad linguistics. The only question that has any bearing on the propriety of a form of speech is: *Is it in reputable use?* And the answer here is that educated people do say *more unique* and *more complete.* [P. 106.]

In England, however, the attitude appears to be different, even taking into consideration the slightly dubious test sentence: *The process is very unique.* This sentence averaged 11 percent acceptance, the lowest of any item surveyed (p. 53).

Less as a substitute for *fewer* is almost uniformly objected to in English textbooks. Evans and Evans take a liberal view in accepting *less than* as a plural while acknowledging that *less* before a plural (*less men*) is not widely accepted:

> A great many people object to it. But a great many others, whose education and position cannot be questioned, see nothing wrong in it. In the United States a college president might speak of less men or less courses. [P. 272.]

In England the test item was *There were* less *road accidents this Christmas than last.* The verdict was 55 percent acceptance for informal speech but a mere 18 percent for formal writing (pp. 49-50).

An historic event is regarded by many as proper use, particularly on the formal level. But Evans and Evans explain that formerly, *h* sounds in *history, hotel,* etc., were not pronounced, and therefore the *an* was natural. "But this is no longer true and these archaic *an's,* familiar from English literature, should not be repeated in modern writing" (p. 3).

To illustrate that even spelling conventions undergo changes at the present and that level of formality can be a factor here, we refer to an item from Mittins: "In spite of the delay, everything was *alright.*" While we have no U.S. data available on this spelling, we predict that Americans, being dictionary-conscious, would reject this spelling in greater percentages than the British. It actually mustered a majority acceptance (55 percent) in informal writing, but less than one-third in formal writing (p. 109).

Connectives

The preposition *between* has for a long time been classified as appropriate only when the object was two things or people. For more than two, *among* was to be used. Pooley marshals an array of evidence, including the *Oxford English Dictionary,* to show that this is too restricting. While it *is* used with two things or people, he says, "its second use is that in which *between* denotes a distinction in several persons or objects considered individually: 'The five diplomats settled the question *between* them' . . ." But *among* would be appropriate in *Divide this among the members of your class.* In brief, the rationale for using *between* with more than two is to distinguish "between any two of a larger number" (p. 131). Evans and Evans take the same view: "We say *the difference between the three men* when we are thinking of each man compared with each of the others, separately and individually. But we would say *the three men quarreled among themselves* because we are then thinking of them as a group of three, and not as a series of pairs" (p. 60). (Consider *Switzerland lies among France, Italy, Austria, and Germany* and the equally unacceptable but informal *Just among you and me and the lamppost. . . .*) On the other side of the Atlantic there was likewise tolerance of *between* for more than two. The test sentence was *The agreement* between *the four powers was cancelled.* With an overall acceptability of 57 percent in the four categories, this ranked eighth from the top out of the 50 usage items with a spread from 67 percent to 32 percent, presumably the difference between informal speech and formal writing (p. 39).

The expressions *is because, is why, is when* sound semi-literate to many people. Pooley quotes reputable writers from

Thoreau to modern critics who use such constructions. He feels that while they should not be forced on those who object to them, there are no grounds for condemning such syntax in either high school or college students, "who are reflecting in its use a natural and common idiom, so far established as to be not eschewed by speakers and writers of respectable attainments" (pp. 128-129). Evans and Evans agree with Pooley, indicating that *is because,* for example, "has been standard English for centuries." They charge that the very grammarians who condemn it use it themselves (p. 56). Mittins observes that Leonard's survey classified the following sentence "disputable": *Intoxication is* when *the brain is affected by certain stimulants,* and the recent survey in England registered even less tolerance—an overall acceptance rate of 37 percent (p. 68).

The phrase *due to* has been condemned as an adverbial modifier. Critics prefer *owing to* or *because of.* Pooley, however, quotes various authorities in support of the usage: Kenyon, while acknowledging his prejudice against it, confesses that it "has staked its claim and squatted in our midst alongside of and in exact imitation of *owing to,* its aristocratic neighbor and respected fellow-citizen" (pp. 136-137). Evans and Evans note that *owing to* and *due to* are grammatically alike and that the latter is used constantly in the adverbial sense (*He failed due to carelessness*) (p. 147). In England, the sentence *The performance ended early, due to illness among the players* received 61 percent approval for informal speech situation, but only 27 percent in formal writing, the overall acceptance being 43 percent.

Some doubt that *if* can be substituted for *whether* in a noun clause expressing uncertainty (*I don't know if he can come*), but again Pooley shows that it can (p. 149). Evans and Evans show that this is only a recent concern and that fifty years ago grammarians saw nothing wrong with it. They say "It never has been restricted in this way and is not now" (p. 231).

Finally, objections have been raised to the use of *than* as a preposition, particularly when it is followed by a personal pronoun (*I'm taller than him*). Pooley shows that *than whom* is "an ancient and respectable form, fully established in

English" and that *than him* or *than her* is acceptable informally in America, but not yet on the formal level (pp. 166-167). Evans and Evans differentiate between two uses of *than* as a preposition. Encountering the sentence *He understands this better than I,* they claim that most speakers would recast it with a "dummy verb": . . . *better than I do.* On the other hand, after a linking verb most who would use the sentence *It is me* would also use *Is she taller than me?* (p. 503). In England the issue seems to be one of the appropriate level of formality. *He is older than me* received a high (78 percent) acceptance for informal speech but a slim (16 percent) acceptance for formal writing (p. 55).

It can be seen from this overview that it is dangerous to take too simplistic a view regarding what is and what is not acceptable. A usage that is unacceptable on the formal level may be perfectly acceptable on the informal level, particularly in speaking. Some constructions that are not acceptable in England may be acceptable in America and vice versa. Moreover, some constructions that were disputable a few decades ago are now quite reputable. Whether adapting a text or deciding how to implement it, one needs to take these usage facts into consideration. At the same time, the teacher should be cautioned against burdening students with a catalog of information on divided usage and Old Wives Tales in the language they are learning. They have far more important matters to concern themselves with, particularly at the beginning and intermediate levels. While the teacher will be on the alert to correct textbook deficiencies at any level, he will need to teach these usage matters in the context of formality and mode—if he undertakes such instruction (on the formal level) at all.

IDIOSYNCRASIES AND SPECIAL DIFFICULTIES

When adapting or selecting what to teach, one should also have in mind the anomalies or peculiarities of the language that might confuse or mislead the student. There are a number of examples in verb tense alone. For example, in American English there is a tendency to use the simple past in preference to the past perfect (*I finished the work before he came*), although the past perfect is required if *when* is incorporated (*He had solved the difficulty when I arrived*). Paul Roberts reminds us that "the future perfect tense is rarely used outside Choice Written English, and not often there" (*He'll leave before we get there* substituting for *He'll have left before we get there*). Shifting to the past tense in reported speech (even with modals) is challenging in any case; but consider the complication that no change is needed if the reporting verb is in the present, present perfect, or future tense. Thus *She'll do it* becomes simply *He says she'll do it.* Time reference in the present perfect tense is subtle. For instance, we can say *They've discussed it recently* but *not They've discussed it yesterday*; we can say *I've worked hard this morning*—provided it is still morning; otherwise we must shift to *I've worked hard today* or *I worked hard this morning.* Additionally, we can say on Friday *They've been relaxing at the beach* since *Monday* but not *They've been relaxing at the beach* since *four days.*

The complexity of English modals presents considerable difficulty for the person learning English. One factor is the multiple meaning of each:

I *must* get there or I'll lose my seat.
You simply *must* see the new play at the University.
He *must* envy you. (deduction)

Absence of necessity requires a different verb (*You don't have to do it*); while the negative (*You* mustn't *worry about it*) changes the meaning to something approaching *shouldn't.* Unlike the *can/could, will/would* combinations, the past deduction can use *must,* but with a perfect verb form (*She must have been tired*). Future deduction also requires a special verb form (unlike *can go, might go,* etc., future deduction incorporates *going to* plus a verb stem—*They must be going to eat*).

As suggested in Chapter 4, two-word verbs are a challenge not only because they are so numerous and because the particle attachment effects such a change in meaning from the original verb stem but also because of the complex rules governing the two types. When a personal pronoun is the object of the verb, it *must* be placed between the verb and the particle (*He called her up*) but not so with inseparable two-word verbs (*I looked for him*).

The rules for English tags are admittedly complex. This is compounded by questions which provide only a feeble cue to the form of the tag:

He's done quite well . . .
She'll do it . . .
I'm quite prompt . . .
He used to live on a farm . . .

In addition, there are some idiosyncrasies (Allen 1959, pp. 166-167):

Stop that noise, will you?
Let's go for a walk, shall we?
He's coming, is he?
I've broken a cup. Oh you have, have you?
I won't eat it. Oh you won't, won't you?
I hate you! You do, do you?

Also in the area of verb rules is the requirement that verb contractions not end a sentence (after *Are you going?* not *Yes, I'm* but rather *Yes, I am*); however, with *not* the contraction is permitted (*Is he going? No, he isn't*).

Collocation of English verbs and verbals presents the learner with what appear to be numerous inconsistencies:

Tell him the answer *but not* Explain him the answer.
I like to fish *but not* I enjoy to fish.
He's having a party *or* She's having a baby *but not* He's having a headache *or* He's having a new car.

We have likewise observed the seeming arbitrary nature of count and noncount nouns:

three pies *but not* three breads
a couch *but not* a furniture

The indefinite *one* also seems arbitrary:

> the other ones *but not* the three ones
> I want this one *but not* (*in American English*) I want these ones.

Notice too the plural convention:

> He paid me five dollars for the job *but not* And on the way home I lost the five *dollars* bill he had just given me.

And consider the problem of the retained object in a modifying clause:

> So your uncle bought you a watch! *but not* Yes, and this is the watch that he bought *it* for me.

Again, prepositional references to time and place may appear arbitrary:

> *in* the evening
> *on* July third
> *at* 5:30
> *in* Asia
> *on* Elm Avenue
> *at* 618 Maple

Likewise it seems illogical that subordinators such as *when* can be used not only with adverb clauses (*He left* when *he was told to*) but also with noun clauses (*I know* when *he left*).

Finally, replies in both the negative and the affirmative are surprisingly varied:

> Will you apologize?   *Never*
> Is she rich?   She has *no* money whatsoever
> Does he like ice cream?   He *hates* it
> Is he sad?   Very!
> Has he quit?   I'm afraid so
> Are you going?   Definitely
> Is he tall?   And how!
> Is it a Ford?   I understand it is

In conclusion, we as language teachers need to be sensitive to those areas in language that are potentially confusing or difficult, just as we need to be up to date on current usage. Such awareness can provide us with the tools for sound textbook adaptation.

SECTION THREE

LANGUAGE VARIETY

CHAPTER 6

CHOOSING THE APPROPRIATE REGISTER

Besides being concerned about contextualization and usage, the language teacher needs to be aware of the many varieties of the language he is teaching and the implications these have when he is adapting textbook lessons for his specific class. These varieties fall into two broad categories: (1) those over which the speaker is expected to have considerable control— adjustments according to the occasion, the relationship between speakers, topic, and medium of communication; and (2) those over which he normally has little or no control— including regional variety, and differences related to speaker age, sex, educational background, or social role. This chapter and the next two deal with implications stemming from both broad categories: namely, the need for appropriate communication and the need to clarify meaning through standardizing or simplifying.

Presently there is broad consensus that communication in a second language involves far more than mere mastery of new vocabulary, syntax, and phonology. Stevick (1971) recognized this several years ago when he postulated his socio-topical matrix in which speaker role and subject were added to the usual linguistic component of the language lesson (pp. 50-54).

SOCIALLY APPROPRIATE INTERACTION

While language texts often identify polite formulas, including request forms, use of the negative, and the like, the majority are deficient in providing cultural guidelines for normal interaction. Appropriate adaptation requires supplementary activity to complement the limited and limiting linguistic data in the text, in order to help generate bona fide communicative competence. In their methods text, Paulston and Bruder (1976) suggest that in second-language instruction, proficiency in social usage is equally as important as proficiency in linguistic usage. Referring to English, they indicate:

> We all teach the WH questions early in the curriculum, but we don't teach the questions you can and cannot ask. If you were to ask me how much money I make, I would probably consider you drunk, mad or shockingly boorish. Yet it is a highly polite question in many Asian countries. [P. 57.]

They further illustrate how ignorance of social rules can seriously impede communication. Paulston says:

> Here is an example from my recent stay in Sweden, where I was born and raised. We (my American husband and children) celebrated Thanksgiving by having my immediate family (Swedish) and friends for a traditional turkey dinner. I was busy in the kitchen and came belatedly into the living room just after my sister-in-law had arrived. In impeccable Swedish I asked her politely, "Do you know everyone?" Any native American would correctly interpret such a question to mean that I wanted to know if she had been introduced to those guests she had not previously met. She looked at me sourly and said, "I don't know everyone, but if you are asking me if I have greeted everyone, I have." Fussed as I was, and in such an archetypical American situation, I had momentarily forgotten that proper Swedish manners demand that guests do not wait to be introduced by a third party, but go around the room, shake hands with everyone and say their name aloud to those they have not previously

met. Any child knows that, so my sister-in-law felt that I had reprimanded her for bad manners, for faulty sharing of a systematic set of social interactional rules. Clearly, the meaning of an interaction is easily misinterpreted if the speakers don't share the same set of rules. Hence the necessity for teaching those rules. [Pp. 57-58.]

In addition, teachers and students should be aware of actions, gestures, and behavior appropriate in the target culture. For instance, at any theater in the Soviet Union (and in some other countries as well), it is extraordinarily rude when passing along a row in front of those seated, to do so (as Americans usually do) with one's back to those he is passing. While it is generally considered appropriate and even desirable for an American husband to kiss his wife or put his arm around her in the presence of his children, such an action would be offensive in a Japanese home. Conversely, Americans feel their personal space is being invaded when someone from an Arab or Latin American country approaches very close

during a conversation. Males holding hands (as is customary among friends in Ethiopia and elsewhere) is misunderstood by Americans; as is the averted gaze and whispered response of some Africans who are simply trying to be polite. The "come here" gesture of Brazilians and other Latins can easily be mistaken by Americans as a farewell gesture; their "I don't know" or "Search me" gesture (finger tips flicked from underneath the chin) appears either rude or meaningless. And the examples can be multiplied in any number of situations ranging from the tendency in some cultures to resist queueing or lining up for service, to procedures in cashing checks, eating dinner, relaxing in an easy chair (the usual posture of American males appears crude to many Eastern Europeans), and even the attire one wears while shopping. The intercultural misunderstanding that regularly results from such nonverbal interaction is of course enormous.

What is the teacher to do when the text largely ignores needed cultural and social interaction activities? One answer for intermediate to advanced students is to provide role-play opportunities. Situations can be selected that focus on the needed social etiquette or area of possible cultural misunderstanding. Participants should be prepared by being provided in writing with full details of the situation and the role they are to assume. Relevant vocabulary or expressions should be discussed ahead of time so that there isn't unnecessary floundering or groping during the role play. Necessary props are provided: a table setting for a meal; money (real or imitation) for a transaction; telephone sets for a phone call. It is important that the role play be acted out so that language is integrated with action and so that appropriate nonverbal actions are mastered simultaneously with the linguistic code. Conversation should be as spontaneous as possible, and the situation should be reasonably realistic—not ever treated as a farce. It is highly appropriate to critique the role play afterwards, with reactions from the student audience as well as from the teacher. Clarity, plausibility, and appropriate actions or gestures would receive the bulk of attention.

Another alternative is the mini-drama. Mini-dramas are useful not only in developing the fluency of participants but also in spotlighting social rules and intercultural problems. Preparation for the mini-drama is similar to that for role play; however, out-of-class rehearsal is appropriate, and the student audience has minimal preparation for the dramatic presentation. Mini-dramas with a cultural focus typically illustrate an intercultural misunderstanding. For example, an American purchasing a money order overseas, is annoyed because people "crowd in" ahead of him and the clerk begins helping others before his transaction is completed. Local people (who don't line up for service) find the American's disgruntled attitude evidence that he wants special attention; and his not moving out of the way after initiating the transaction is seen as selfish and arrogant. Following the mini-drama, class members discuss the probable causes of misunderstanding.

Other activities include talking one's way out of trouble, problem solving, panel discussions, and interviews with native speakers. (For further suggestions, see Kettering 1975, and Rivers 1972.) In brief, socially appropriate interaction can be taught both by acting out relevant material from the text and by initiating supplementary activities. The latter can include reference to questions and topics unsuitable in the target culture or country, and therefore to be avoided.

SOCIALLY APPROPRIATE LANGUAGE—REGISTER

To this point in our discussion of appropriateness, we have been primarily concerned with *what* should be said and done in a communicative situation. We now turn to *how* this might be carried out, depending on a variety of circumstances. These circumstances include not only the occasion and the subject but also the relative status of the speakers and their acquaintance, not to mention their attitude toward each other and toward the subject being discussed. One further "circumstance" is the medium of communication—oral or written; this will be considered later in the chapter.

The changing form our communication takes as we move from one set of circumstances to another is sometimes referred to as *register*. Halliday, McIntosh, and Strevens (1964) note that "the choice of items from the wrong register and the mixing of different registers, are among the most frequent mistakes made by a nonnative speaker of a language" (p. 88).

We recall the occasion when we reminded a very polite and eager-to-please foreign student that her homework was again overdue. Smiling sweetly, she gently responded, "So what."

Contemporary language texts, striving to escape the bland language and stereotyped situations of the past decades, are beginning to provide colorful, idiomatic language spoken by believable or even off-beat characters in interesting settings. An exercise from a very recent text provides practice in contradicting:

> I can't see.   You can too see!
> She didn't forget.   She did forget!
> (etc.)

However, it provides no caution as to the circumstances under which this exchange would be appropriate. The same text includes a slightly abrasive dialogue followed by related drill:

> *Jackson*: You didn't think I'd leave him behind, did you?
> *Addy*:   Quite honestly, it wouldn't surprise me in the least.
>
> *Addy*:   Pay attention, Jackson; have your ticket ready.
> *Jackson*: Really, Addy! Don't you think I can read!

While the speaker is referred to as "straightforward" in the drill, again no suggestions or guidelines are provided on how and when to use such utterances.

In another language text, frank, colloquial language is employed in a statement-reply drill:

> I believe you'll eventually apologize to Susan.
> That's what you think. I wouldn't apologize to Susan on a bet.
>
> Jack claims you're going to Alaska.
> That's what he thinks. I wouldn't go to Alaska on a bet.
>
> They say Frank will join the Army.
> That's what they think. He wouldn't join the Army on a bet.

Joan thinks Mr. Adams will dismiss class.
That's what she thinks. He wouldn't dismiss class on a
   bet.

There are some obvious pluses: Students receive practice in the
often-neglected area of responding to statements. Grammar
and phonological matters are provided situationally. And we
have unusually natural-sounding samples of speech in substantive, interesting, contemporary conversation.

The most serious limitation of this drill is the lack of any
guidance regarding when and with whom to use these
rejoinders. It is not inconceivable that a student who had
mastered this drill would unsettle a teacher or employer with
an inappropriate *That's what you think*. The genuine idiomatic
character of the response heightens the lack of congruence
when not used appropriately: One instinctively expects that a
speaker with such a linguistic repertoire has comparable
sophistication in when to use these expressions.

Another limitation of drills in the text from which the
example was taken is that many are highly colloquial, full of
slang, and intimate or good-naturedly flippant; alternate
responses are not provided. The result is that these replies
often sound "cute," curious, or simply incongruous in the
speech of nonnative speakers. In addition, some of the drills
provide rather low-frequency responses—in other words, replies that are idiomatic but only occasionally employed in
everyday speech.

There are various ways to improve on such drills. For one
thing, the setting and identification of the speakers should be
clearly indicated. It would also be helpful to identify
situations in which the response would be *in*appropriate.
Suitable alternate responses for these situations should also be
provided, notably "common denominator" responses appropriate in a variety of circumstances. Then too, the drills could
easily be edited; those expressions that seem too "cute" or
seldom used could be omitted. A sample revision follows:

Situation 1: Walking back to the dorm after class. The
speaker is a roommate about your age, a person you
know well.

Your roommate: I believe you'll eventually apologize to Susan.

You: That's what you think. I wouldn't apologize to her on a bet.

Situation 2: At school after class; a friendly chat. The speaker is your teacher, an older person, one that you respect but don't know well personally yet.

Class discussion of possible responses (student suggestions):

No way!	(Abrupt)
You've gotta be kidding.	(Familiar)
You're probably right.	(No, probably hypocritical)
Do you think so?	(A possibility; we can build on this)

Your teacher: I believe you'll eventually apologize to Susan.

You: Do you think so? Right now I don't think I ever will.

One open-ended exercise which can help prepare students for responses suited to the occasion (e.g., a friendly chat as above), the interlocutor (varied), and attitude toward subject (strength of feeling) is a five-level response to statements and questions. The student hears a statement and then is required to make one of the following responses:

1   strong agreement
2   mild agreement
3   noncommittal response
4   mild disagreement
5   strong disagreement

In sum, to adapt exercises so that the student can learn to tailor the appropriate register of the language to the situation, the teacher should give attention to those of the following variables that he feels are critical to the communication:

1. The setting (e.g., one-on-one conversation or small group communication; in person or over the phone; quiet or noisy background, etc.)

2. The occasion (e.g., conversation, argument, narration; dinner, reception, funeral, etc.)
3. The subject of discussion (e.g., formula greetings or exchanges, intimate or domestic topic, technical subject, etc.)
4. Relationship among speakers (e.g., status of interlocutor, how well he is known by the speaker, degree of cordiality, etc.)

Interfacing with these is the appropriate level of formality. These categories range from the simple formal-informal dichotomy to Gleason's (1965) five-level scale:

5	oratorical
4	deliberative
3	consultative
2	casual
1	intimate

(Also see Joos 1962, and Chapter 9 of this volume.) While the foreign speaker will probably never have occasion to employ the ornate *oratorical* form, he might on rare occasions appropriately use the careful, rather precise *deliberative* register, if addressing a fair-sized group of people—particularly if he is not well acquainted with them and the occasion is serious or the subject is technical. In a small group situation where the speaker is not too well acquainted with the others, he would probably adopt the more informal *consultative* level, with its shorter sentences and loose grammatical style. In a one-on-one situation, and especially with those he knows well and feels entirely comfortable with, he would be inclined to use the sometimes clipped or slangy *casual* key: "Hafta take off so soon?" The *intimate* level is normally reserved for one's immediate family and personal domestic situations, and is rarely needed by a second-language learner.

It would of course be an unnecessary burden for the student to master the labels in the taxonomy just described. We recommend again a situational orientation: for example, talking about marriage plans with one's brother, discussing a recent soccer match with roommates one knows well, planning a class project with a newly-formed student committee, purchasing a new jacket, discussing a visa problem with a university official, giving a talk or participating in a panel discussion on TV ("Coping with Adjustment Problems of Foreign Students on American Campuses"), or appealing a traffic ticket to a student court. The initial presentation of relevant vocabulary and idioms and of a sample dialog (adapted if possible from the textbook) would be followed by one-on-one or small group practice and then role play. Critiques and summary would pinpoint differences in register among the various situations. Participants would identify the factors contributing to the different registers employed.

THE BORN LOSER   by Art Sansom

As students develop increasing awareness of the appropriate register that should be used with varying situations, they will need help in becoming consistent in the use of a given register. This can be furthered by providing examples to supplement the text. Intermediate students can occasionally prepare a dialog to suit a particular situation, and they can adapt a reading selection to a dialog format. Some of these could be recorded; and all would be checked for consistency. The teacher can likewise adapt textbook or dialogs; native informants can be invited to dramatize specific situations. A variety of illustrative material can be collected, ranging from comic strips and stories containing dialog to specially prepared supplementary materials (such as Morley 1972, McConochie 1975, Hines 1973, Velder et al. 1973, 1976, Via 1975a and b, Bodman and Lanzano 1975, Oxford University Press 1973, and Kettering 1975).

One further dimension of register, or appropriate language use, is the matter of propriety. We recently had some overseas English teachers come to us to resolve a minor dispute. One of these capable nonnative English speakers had visited a Commonwealth country. While there he picked up the use of the expletive *bloody*. His colleagues were offended by this expression, but he insisted they were prudish and out of date. We noted that the word in question has little emotive effect on Americans, since they normally use it only as a simple adjective. A. S. Hornby points out that even when used as a slang expression, some words such as *bloody* have varying impact depending on the context and also depending on the audience. These expressions, then, should be avoided or used only when the nonnative speaker is fully confident they are acceptable to his audience.

Since we have recommended drawing upon a variety of sources to supplement the text that fails to provide exposure to various registers of the language, it is important for the teacher to sensitize his students to taboo words and offensive language. These words and phrases are carefully marked in the excellent British *Advanced Learner's Dictionary*. The editor (Hornby 1974) comments:

These are taboo words which may be met, particularly in contemporary prose and drama, but which it is best not to use. The likelihood is that you will cause consternation. These words were never heard outside extremely vulgar contexts unless used in a meaningless sense in coarse colloquial style. There used to be a ban on the use of such words, particularly in print or on radio and television. Today the ban has been lifted and these words are often heard or seen. This does not mean that their use has become generally acceptable. The foreign learner of English may need to understand them but will do well to avoid using them, especially in conversation. [P. *xi.*]

To enliven their texts, some authors introduce slang expressions. The teacher-adapter again needs to provide guidance on the appropriate use of slang. It is common only in casual and intimate speech, or highly informal or colloquial writing. Evans and Evans (1957) note that while some slang is witty and dynamic, the majority is

merely faddish and infantile and its consistent use does not display the fullness of expression that the user thinks it does but rather a triteness and a staleness that the user is apparently unaware of. Slang ages quickly and nothing so stamps a total lack of force or originality upon a man or woman as the steady use of outmoded slang. [P. 458.]

In brief, the student needs to use slang selectively and sparingly. Even with these cautions, it is likely to be misused. Probably in no other area of the language is the advanced student so susceptible to error. The lure to use slang seems almost irresistible since it appears to be the ultimate achievement—the trademark of the native speaker. But slang is fickle: not only is it rapidly dated, but the teenage native speaker informant may provide an expression that sounds childishly inappropriate in the mouth of the thirty-year-old language learner; and the middle-aged informant may provide a regional or obsolete example. While dictionaries and informants can help, the best guide (other than abstinence or moderation) is a carefully tuned ear to the use of slang by a variety of people in a number of situations.

LANGUAGE APPROPRIATE TO THE MEDIUM

One exercise that appears in a variety of language textbooks requires the student to rewrite a prose passage. For example, he may be asked to make grammatical changes such as changing a series of questions to statements, active to passive, third person to first person, etc. He sometimes is asked to transform indirect address to direct address or a narrative passage to a dialog. The latter assignment rarely takes into account the differences that exist between the written and the oral expression of an idea. To be sure, obvious differences in tense (*He said that he was coming.* / *"I'm coming."*) as well as connectives and reporting speech are pointed out; moreover, punctuation differences are noted and sometimes drilled. But the student is generally unaware of the more significant differences that typify the written and spoken modes of expression.

In their comprehensive grammar, Quirk, Greenbaum, Leech, and Svartvik (1973) observe these differences and identify two principal causes: the first is situational—a presumption that the person being addressed is not present. Unable to receive clarification questions or gestures of assurance that the message is being understood, the writer is inclined to be more precise and careful than the speaker; the fact that the message can be examined repeatedly likewise makes for more cautious expression in order to avoid criticism. A second difficulty, they argue, is the inability to represent tempo, intonation, and our great repertoire of nonverbal adjuncts. This can result in a shift from the simply phrased verbal utterance *John didn't do it* (with a particular intonation nucleus on *John*) to an elaborated written version: *It was not in fact John that did it* (p. 22). Bailey (1973) elaborates on both of these limitations:

> This transition from speech to writing presents a variety of difficulties beyond the obvious ones of symbolizing the spoken language according to the conventions of English spelling. In several ways, the written language is impoverished: it lacks any mechanism for representing gesture and tone of voice that provide so much support

for speech, and it requires the writer to create for himself the sense of an audience that is normally supplied in conversation by the interaction between speaker and listener. As anyone knows who has tried to write dialogue for a story or a play, the illusion of naturalness is extremely difficult to create. Even the transcript of a telephone conversation where gestures play no part, is quite unlike the imitation of such a conversation in fiction. The sense of an audience is at once a normal part of our spoken language behavior and an extremely difficult thing to capture in writing. [P. 395.]

The second-language learner who has relied heavily on the textbook can encounter fully as much difficulty in developing fluency in the *oral* medium.

A British colleague confided that after fourteen years abroad, he was told by friends in England that he "spoke like a book." All too many "advanced" second-language learners "speak like books." The fault, as we have hinted in Chapters 1, 2, and 3, can often be traced to textbook presentations which fail to differentiate between the written and spoken medium. The following are representative weaknesses in conversation exercises or dialogs:

Example	*Weakness*
1. I have not seen him all morning.	Reluctance to use contractions
2. Do the Smiths go fishing in the summer? Yes, they often go fishing in the summer.	Compulsion to require full-sentence replies
3. For whom was he looking?	Reluctance to end a sentence with a preposition; the result, rather formal-sounding speech
4. Something is feasible. The highway could be completed in two weeks. That the highway could be completed in two weeks is feasible.	Practice with structures unlikely in most speech situations

5. Have you ever seen anything like that before?

Absence in many texts of ellipses or abbreviated sentences so common in intimate or casual speech, and sometimes in informal speech:
"Ever seen anything like that before?"

6. Do you think your automatic choke could be stuck?
Yes, it might be stuck.

Failure to provide for normal interaction when possible confusion might occur:
"What's an 'automatic choke'?"
(And by the way, how would I get it unstuck?)

7. What country are you from?
I'm from Taiwan.
Have you ever visited Japan?
Yes, I have.

Inadequate provision for responding to *statements*:
"I'm from Taiwan."
"I see. I've never been there, but I have been to Japan and the Philippines."
"Is that so? I stopped in Osaka and Tokyo on the way to the States."

8. She skipped her French class yesterday.
No, she didn't.

Little provision for attuning the student to various degrees of social interaction: noncommittal responses, gentle doubt, alternate possibilities—to shocked surprise or indignant rejection of an idea:
"She skipped class yesterday."
"Is that so?"
"What makes you think that?"
"That doesn't sound like Debbie."
"Maybe she wasn't feeling well."
"I thought I saw her in class."
"Are you sure? She never misses class."
"Oh, that's terrible. She was scheduled to give a report in my place."
"She did not! She sat next to me all period."

9. Did you say they miss you?
/did yuw sey ðey mis yuw/

Inadequate attention to stress, intonation, assimilation, reduction, etc.:
/dijuw sey ðey mišuw/

10. Unintentionally rapid:
We-would-like-to-provide-these-mature-intelligent-adults-with-English-instruction-which-is-intellectually-challenging-but-at-the-same-time-remains-within-the-constraints-of-their-limited-capabilities-in-English.

Neglect in dialogs and exercises of the means for the listener to interrupt in order to have the speaker slow down, speak louder, or repeat a phrase

11. Nonverbal communication.

Neglect of nonverbal responses or requests *in place* of verbal utterances, for example, when speaking out in a meeting might be disruptive or difficult to be heard. Consider nonverbal cues for:
"I can't hear."
"It doesn't matter to me."
"There are two (seats) here."
"Hello, Ann."
"It's time to go."

As indicated earlier, the transition from oral to written communication is likewise challenging. However, for the learner who is literate in his own language, the acquisition of effective oral communication in the foreign tongue will probably constitute the greater challenge. He will be significantly aided by the teacher who is fully aware of the differences in these two media and is willing to adapt his teaching materials accordingly.

Adaptation of the type discussed in this chapter will normally require the teacher to *supplement* his text in order to free the student from a restricted, often bookish, code. This will in turn enable the learner to communicate appropriately in a variety of contexts.

CHAPTER 7
STANDARDIZATION

As the nonnative speaker develops greater communicative proficiency, he can be expected to produce an increasing range of situationally appropriate language. The previous chapter concentrated on how to achieve needed flexibility in this area. We now turn our attention to other language differences that the student will need to cope with, but primarily in a passive rather than an active manner. These include language differences according to age, sex, or geographical region as well as differences stemming from educational or social background and temporal variety.

AGE AND SEX DIFFERENCES IN LANGUAGE

All languages tend to reflect age and sex differences among native speakers. Generally there is little or no difficulty in deciphering meaning through these differences; indeed, on the written level particularly, it is usually impossible to perceive the sex of the writer. The primary need of the language learner, then, is simply to avoid acquiring language characteristics inappropriate to his or her age or sex.

We sometimes smile at how typical it is for a toddler to begin climbing atop furniture or for a child to splash through a puddle of water. And child language is virtually as distinctive from that of adults as is the difference in activities of the two groups. Early phrasal utterances and grammatical simplification need no illustration. But even after a significant lexical corpus and all of the basic syntax have been acquired, the language of children is distinctive. Consider J. D. Salinger's representation of the speech of young Phoebe, a girl of elementary school age:

> "[The play] starts out when I'm dying. This ghost comes in on Christmas Eve and asks me if I'm ashamed and everything. You know. For betraying my country and everything. Are you coming to it? ... That's what I wrote you about. Are you?" [1945, P. 146.]

> ... "I'm going with you. Can I? Okay ... I took [my suitcase] down the back elevator so Charlene wouldn't see me. It isn't heavy. All I have in it is two dresses and my moccasins and my underwear and socks and some other things. Feel it. It isn't heavy. Feel it once ... Can't I go with you? Holden? Can't I? *Please.*" [P. 185.]

We notice immediately the repetition and the frequent use of coordinators. Sentences are typically short or, if longer, a series of clauses spliced together with *and* or *so* or *but*. In addition there are some nouns (*mommy*), adjectives (*teeny*), and rather transitory expletives (*Neato!*) that characterize the speech of many children. Slang is quite visible, as a rule, and there is sometimes even a saltiness reflecting increasing permissiveness in entertainment media.

Teenagers, as we know, have acquired greater adaptability to varying social situations. In medium-sized peer groups, there is often an increased use of slang, telescoped sentences, esoteric expressions, and even intentionally ungrammatical usage—for the sake of humor or to identify with the group. Bel Kaufman provides us a sample (almost a caricature) of high school speech replete with these characteristics:

> Hi, teach!
> Looka her! She's a teacher?
> . . .
> Hey she's cute! Hey, teach, can I be in your class?
> . . .
> O, no! A *dame* for homeroom?

You want I should slug him, teach?

. . .

What's your name?
My name is on the board.
I can't read your writing.
I gotta go to the nurse. I'm dying.
Don't believe him, teach. He ain't dying!

. . .

When do we go home?
The first day of school, he wants to go home already!
I'd like you to come to order, please. I'm afraid we won't have time for the discussion on first impressions I had planned. I'm passing out—
Hey, she's passing out!
Give her air!
—Delaney cards. You are to fill them out at once. . . .
In ink or pencil?
I got no ink—can I use pencil? Who's got a pencil to loan me?
I don't remember when I was born.
Don't mind him—he's a comic.
Print or write?
When do we go to lunch?
I can't write upside down!
Ha-ha. He kills me laughing!
What do you need my address for? My father can't come.
Someone robbed my ball-point!
I can't do it—I lost my glasses. [1964, Pp. 13-15.]

The teacher whose language learners are exposed to realistic speech samples of young children or adolescents may well need to adapt their language or reading instruction in one or more of the following ways: explain the meaning of idiomatic expressions, identify ungrammatical expressions, discuss situations with cultural implications, and indicate relative ranges of various expressions. Adult language learners should of course be cautioned against using specific items characteristic of children and adolescents.

Some feminists might want to challenge the assertion that there are language features peculiar to the speech of women, but it is widely recognized that there are certain lexical and even some phonological items that are used more frequently by females than by males. The degree of difference varies from language to language. Goldschmidt (n.d.) identifies an Indian tribe in Brazil in which male and female speech differ significantly. Halliday notes that such differences are more prominent in Japanese, for instance, than in either English or Chinese:

> There is even some formal difference in Japanese between the speech of men and the speech of women, nor is this merely a difference in the probabilities of occurrence. In most languages some lexical items tend to be used more by one sex than the other; but in Japanese there are grammatical features which are restricted to the speech of one sex only. [Halliday et al. 1964, p. 24.]

We have noted elsewhere that this difference can also be observed in Spanish, where for example a woman *but not a man* can say *"Estoy contenta"* (Bowen 1966, pp. 35-44).

Differences in male and female speech are likewise functions of speaker age, social situation, and time. Our impression, verified informally by others, is that the word *cute* is used more frequently by women than by men to express approbation. The latter might employ it in reference to a baby or the dress of a little girl, while many women use it in a wider variety of contexts. Very young girls and many teenage girls appear to use it more frequently than do their mothers in such male contexts as *She has the cutest boyfriend!*

Not only has the role of women changed since World War II (women moving into "men's" jobs and professional roles), but they have been gaining legal and even "lexical" equality (e.g., *Ms.* and *chairperson*). Part of the nonsexist language trend has been a rejection by many women of the diminutives, dainty expletives, and discreet euphemisms of the previous generation. Thus this post-World War II transcript of a male speaking "female language" now sounds like a dated chauvinistic caricature of an older woman:

> I don't want to be catty, but my dear it was simply too terrible. I really thought I should have died. I just wanted

to sink right through the floor. My gracious me, I thought
of Burt and Charlie wearing that same cunning homburg
hat. [Goldschmidt.]

Nevertheless, there continue to be differences.[1] Those males
who enjoy earthy language and profanity adjust their language
when women are present—except for female associates who
now regard it as sophisticated or modern. And a large
percentage of women continue to use words that for decades
have been largely restricted to their sex: certain nouns
(*tummy*; *perspiration* more exclusively than *sweat*, although
sweaty is common nowadays), certain adjectives (a *darling* pair
of shoes), and mild expletives (*goodness, heavens*).

As we have said, there are even subtle phonological
differences. Bailey and Robinson (1973) cite a 1967 study
which illustrates this point:

> The use of [n] for [ŋ] in words like *talking, working*
> and *learning* is sometimes a distinctive contrast between
> the English used by men and that used by women. In the
> Detroit Dialect Survey, for example, Shuy and his
> associates found that middle class women used [n] for
> [ŋ] in 15.3 per cent of the possible occurrences, whereas
> men from the same class made the substitution in 63.8
> per cent. Similar contrasts between men and women were
> found for other social classes. [P. 37.]

William Labov's (1966) landmark study on the social
stratification of English provides an additional dimension to
the difference between male and female speech. Interestingly,
the speech of the working class in New York City is associated
"with cultural norms of masculinity." A slim majority of the
men in this speech community favor New York speech, but
women here, showing "much greater linguistic insecurity than
men," have strong negative attitudes toward it (pp. 482-503).
Apparently it is felt that it is logical for men to use masculine
speech but highly inappropriate for women to do so. This
sense of masculinity or femininity extends even into the
realms of national speech differences and speech differences
according to educational level: standard British speech and the

speech of the educated are judged by many Americans to lack virility.

What implications does all this have for those teaching a second language? First, that there are unmistakable differences between the speech of men and women; and also that it is generally unacceptable for those of one sex to use the sexually distinctive linguistic repertoire of the other. Except for occasional slang or idiomatic expressions, comprehension is seldom a problem. Passive recognition of sex differences in speech is sufficient. The problem of students' picking up expressions inappropriate to their sex will probably increase between the intermediate and advanced levels when they are exposed to a broader range of reading material. Adaptation can consist primarily in monitoring the reading, speech, and writing of language learners and advising against the use of inappropriate expressions.

ADAPTING TO REGIONAL AND NATIONAL DIFFERENCES

Regional and national differences in a given language, such as English, tend to be most visible phonologically; but of course there are lexical and occasional structural differences as well. An additional source of variety is the disparity between what we might call "propriety standards" of large urban centers and those in small towns, especially those quite removed from urban centers. For instance, there is little restriction in the language that might be employed in a Broadway theatrical production, but the same language might be highly offensive if used on stage in a town in Nebraska or Tennessee. Obviously language learners in major urban areas who are exposed to such language can benefit by pointers on when to use what.

The teacher will be wise to present only the dialect of the language he is fluent in. This may necessitate occasional departure from a text representing a different (probably standard) dialect. If the language learner is residing in an area where a nonstandard dialect of the target language is spoken, the teacher should probably present both the local and standard form that the student will need to use.

Marckwardt illustrates U.S. variants of a lexical item:

> Let us take *cottage cheese* as an example. This could very well be called the standard form for the home-made cheese that is generally made by allowing curdled milk to stand and then straining it. Now, in eastern New England this is called *sour-milk cheese*; in the inland North, the part I come from, it is *Dutch cheese*; in the Hudson valley, which is a subsection of this, it's *pot cheese. Smear case,* which we borrowed from the Pennsylvania German . . . , is current in a belt running from East to West in the middle of the country. And in the South, I think probably one would find *clabber cheese* or *bonny clabber cheese.* [Marckwardt and Quirk 1964, p. 65.]

But regional differences are not likely to cause much difficulty for the language learner unless he encounters such unusual dialect variants as the following examples of contemporary English:

> YORKSHIRE MAN. Eeh! As far back as I can tell ther's allus bin trouble wi' t' roof o' yond laithe when it rains; t' watter pours in at t' top, at t' riggin', tha knaws, an 't spoutin's rotten. I wa' nobbut a lad about six or seven when my father saw it an' said it 'ld fall down sooin; but it's still theere.
>
> GLOUCESTERSHIRE MAN. As far back as I can mind, there've always been trouble with the roof of that barn when it do rain; the water pours in at the top, at the crease, now, and the shootins is rotten. I were only a boy about six or zeven when me vader zeed'n and said'n would fall down zoon; but he still be there. [Ibid., pp. 60-61.]

Still more difficult is pidgin-English, which appears in such varied areas as Hawaii, New Guinea, and Nigeria. This example is of the African variety:

> "What about Chief Dr Mrs?" I threw in mischievously.
> "That one no sweet for mouth," said the Minister. "E no catch."

"Wetin wrong with am?" asked Mrs John. "Because no woman get am e no go sweet for mouth. I done talk say no only for election time woman de get equality for dis our country."

"No be so, madam," said the journalist. "You no see how the title rough like sand-paper for mouth: 'Dr Chief Mrs.,' E no catch at all." [Achebe 1967, p. 18.]

As with poetry, hearing dialect or pidgin read aloud can aid understanding. In addition, some glossing and occasional paraphrasing in standard English may also be necessary.

Most creoles, on the other hand, would need to be rewritten in the standard dialect in order to be comprehended. Consider this Jamaican creolized form of English:

Hinsed den, "ma, a we in lib?' Hie sie, "Mi no nuo, mi pikini, bot duon luk fi hin niem hahd, ohr eni wie in a di wohld an yu kal di niem, hin hie unu.' Hin sed, "Wel Ma, mi want im hie mi a nuo mi.' 'Lahd nuo, masa! Duo no kal di niem, hin wi kom kil yu.' Hin sie, "Wel Ma, hin wi haf fi kil mi.'

(He said then, "Ma, and where does he live?' She says, 'I don't know, my child, but don't look hard for his name, or anywhere in all the world that you call the name, he will hear you.' He said, "Well, Ma, I want him to hear me and know me.' 'Lord, no, master! Do not call the name: he will come and kill you.' He says, 'Well, Ma, he will have to kill me.') [Quirk et al. 1972, p. 27.]

Perhaps an even greater challenge to language teachers is learning to adapt an entire textbook which employs a *national* dialect different from his own. He will need to cope with cultural differences as well as differences in phonology and occasional lexical and syntactic variants. Below is a sample exercise from a British text.

Responses to have *questions*:
Answer the following questions.

1. Have you a pen?   (sketch of a pen)
       (*Yes, I have a pen.*)
2. How many pencils has James?   (sketch of two pencils)

3. Has Mr. Andrews an automobile?   (sketch of a car)
4. What kind of automobile has Mr. Andrews?

(sketch showing make)

5. Have you a cat or a dog?   (sketch of a dog)
6. How many English books have you?   (sketch of five books)

Here concentrated practice is provided in responding to questions involving *have*. Previously in the lesson this verb was used in statements, and in the following lesson it will be used in the negative. The pictures aid in comprehension—particularly in comprehending new objects being introduced.

If this textbook is used by an American in a setting which permits either British or American English to be taught, he should adapt the exercise to reflect his own speech. In making the adaptation he will need to eliminate item 5 or mark it for intonation, since it is ambiguous as is: The correct answer could be either *A dog* or *Yes* depending on intonation. Finally, full-sentence replies should not be required, especially for yes-no questions. Here is a sample adaptation of exercise:

Answer the following questions.
1. Have you a pen?   (British)[2]   (sketch of a pen)
    (*Yes, I have.*)
  Do you have a pen?   (American)
    (*Yes, I do.*)
  Have you got a pen?   (Br. or Am.)
    (*Yes, I have.*)
2. How many pencils does James have?   (sketch of two pencils)
    (*He has two* [pencils].)

3. Has Mr. Andrews got a car?   (sketch showing make)
4. What kind of car does Mr. Andrews have?   (sketch showing make)

5. Have you got a cat or a dog?   (sketch of a dog)
6. How many English books do you have?   (sketch of five books)

Early on the elementary level of instruction, it would be best to introduce only one question form for *have.* Since *do* is used with most verbs, *do (you) have* is the form that would be used. This creates a limitation for the previous exercise, however, since the students' reply to *Do you have a pencil?* would simply be *Yes* or *Yes, I do.* Thus the *have* form would not be actively practiced. To eliminate this problem, we can use question words: e.g., *How many cars does Mr. Benning have? / He has two (cars).* If students inquire whether or not the simple response *Two* is appropriate to the last question, the teacher should assure them it is, but that for the moment she prefers the short-form reply shown. An acceptable alternative, of course is a one-word or phrasal response followed by a sentence: *Two. He has two VW's.*[3]

ADAPTING TO EDUCATIONAL AND SOCIAL DIFFERENCES

We now recognize that it is naive to consider regional or national differences as though the language in a particular geographical area were of a single variety. Language even in a given city naturally reflects educational and social differences as well as differences in age, sex, national background, and the like.

Interestingly, highly educated speech with its extensive vocabulary, absence of grammatical errors, occasional allusions, etc., can ostracize a speaker from a group that regards such speech as pretentious or lacking in masculinity. In this connection, Shuy (1973) reflects on the time when he was working his way through college as a laborer in a tire manufacturing company. At that time, he said,

> the importance of language in relating to one's fellow employees was never more clear to me. My job involved manufacturing tire treads on a machine which engaged a crew of five other men. My pay was based on how much we as a crew produced in a given evening while my fellow workers were paid at a constant hourly rate, regardless of what we produced. Since I was also a graduate student in English at that time, my role was obviously precarious from the perspective of the other members of my crew, none of whom had finished high school. Whatever else could be deduced from the situation, it was clear beyond words that it was necessary for me to speak something other than grad school English. Since my paycheck was at their mercy, it was obvious that the speech of a grad student simply would not do on the assembly line. This was not a new situation for me, however, for almost all males who grew up in working-class communities can probably remember their adolescent need to speak with masculinity, particularly if there was any question whatsoever about their physical prowess, their ability as athletes, or if they were tortured by the anomaly of a relatively late development of facial hair and deeper voice. Masculinity, they discovered, could be expressed by a choice of vocabulary, grammar, and pronunciation even after their bodies had unceremoniously failed them. [P. 304.]

A second-language teacher whose students have acquired a nonstandard dialect which seems to her ears "uneducated" should consider the advisability of adding a standard variety in order to provide social or economic mobility. Assuming that the nonstandard dialect is useful in his present vocational or social circumstances, the student's usage should certainly not be labeled as incorrect, nor should there be any attempt to eradicate his nonstandard speech. It *would* be necessary, however, for him to learn to be consistent within each of his two registers or dialects.

Social and ethnic differences in language often reflect educational characteristics as well. Notice the dramatic difference between the Harlem dialect of an older Black woman in the first passage and the standard educated English of a Black writer from Tennessee in the second:

"Wait, le'me tell you. I'm laying up there moaning and groaning when here come Lucy and she's in one of her talking moods. Soon as I seen her I knowed pretty soon she was going to want to talk 'bout that bag and I truly dreaded telling her that I'd done looked into it without her. I says, 'Baby, I don't feel so good. You talk to me later' . . . But y'all think that stopped her? Shucks, all she does is to go get me a bottle of cold beer she done brought me and start to running her mouth again. And, just like I knowed she was gon' do, she finally got round to talking 'bout that bag. What ought we to buy *first*, she wants to know. Lawd, that pore chile, whenever she got her mind set on a thing! Well suh, I took me a big swoller of beer and just lay there like I was thinking awhile. [Ellison 1975, p. 104.]

I was to learn that White authors, as well as Afro-American authors, are neglected by the American university. Before I arrived at Berkeley, there was no room in the curriculum for detective novels or Western fiction, even though some of the best contributions to American literature occur in these genres. At another major university, the library did not carry books by William Burroughs, who at least manages to get it up beyond the common, simple, routine narrative that critics become so thrilled about. . . . I suspect that the inability of some students to "understand" works by Afro-American authors is traceable to an inability to understand the American experience as rooted in slang, dialect, vernacular, argot, and all of the other putdown terms the faculty uses for those who have the gall to deviate from the true and proper way of English. [Reed 1975, p. 79.]

The point here is that although distinctive linguistic characteristics of a dialect such as Black English have been identified, these are modified by such factors as region, age, and purpose of communication; moreover, a standard dialect can be acquired for certain purposes to replace or supplement the vernacular dialect.

Also, as Labov and others have noted, the characteristics of language within even a very limited region can vary substantially among social levels in that area. The language teacher whose students are exposed to some of these varieties either through their reading or through interaction within the community can scarcely ignore the possible confusion that might arise. But it is important to bear in mind that elaborate classifications of language variety and interrelationships within this variety are of little or no concern to the second-language learner. For such a person, two things only are important: one, avoiding usage that for him would be inappropriate; and two, receiving assistance when necessary in grasping the meaning of various language varieties that he is exposed to.

The first is ideally handled on an individual basis. But the second—language varieties which confuse or fail to communicate adequately—can be, at least partially, adapted and presented to an entire class. Even those students who can manage the unsimplified language of popular journals and newspapers will find it difficult to fathom prose with very much slang or local dialect in it. Yet they will be bombarded with these "irregularities" on the advanced level and when residing where the target language is spoken. Movies, TV, advertisements, casual conversation, song lyrics, and literature can all prove confusing when seasoned with colloquial and nonstandard speech which most second-language learners have not been exposed to.

To dramatize the effect of educational-social-regional variety in impeding communication for nonnative speakers, we have selected a literary piece which has been adapted and filmed. More difficult than the prose the foreign student would normally encounter, this excerpt from an Uncle Remus tale can serve as a catalyst to consider various ways in which a piece might be adapted in order to increase the nonnative speaker's comprehension of it. The tale begins:

> One time, after Brer Rabbit done bin trompin' roun' huntin' up some sallid fer ter make out he dinner wid, he fine hisse'f in de neighborhoods er Mr. Man house, en he

> pass 'long twel he come ter de gyardin-gate, en nigh de gyardin-gate he see Little Gal playin' roun' in de san' . . . [Harris 1955, p. 126.]

In addition to the challenging dialect and errors in standard usage, the author complicates the spelling by attempting a somewhat phonetic representation of many words that have a characteristic dialect pronunciation (e.g., *en* for *and*; *sallid* for *salad*, etc.)

What are some possible solutions? One that immediately suggests itself is the total avoidance of this kind of writing in the second-language class. Perhaps this extreme solution is advisable for a group of engineering students whose only need for English is to read reference articles in their professional field. But we would be most reluctant to completely ignore Joel Chandler Harris in a course on American literature or area studies. It is rich and typical, some of the best of American creative fiction, and because of its African background, valuable in a program of comparative literature.

A less extreme solution would be to edit dialog of this difficulty. Another, for teachers who are fluent in reading such material orally, would be to have students listen to a live or taped presentation. Related visuals, such as flannel board figures, could help with the story line. For advanced students, a few excerpts might be written out with the spelling regularized, but no other changes. Another possibility would be to regularize the language of these excerpts in order to further clarify the meaning. Still another alternative would be to simplify the language and gloss over unfamiliar words or expressions. But here a caution is in order. Students would need to be told that most of the charm of the story stems from the language of the narrator; therefore, any adaptation should be regarded only as a temporary expedient to help the reader grasp the meaning and the conventions utilized by the author. But even when the meaning is clear, these tales must be heard to be fully appreciated. Hearing them helps reveal the folksy, thigh-slapping, mock-serious good humor of the narrator. Like ballads and song lyrics, they should be read for understanding, but they should also be listened to for fuller appreciation.

Finally, certain explanations can help: The narrator is a kindly old Black (Uncle Remus) whose affection for little children prompts him to entertain them with his imaginative tales. He uses certain conventions such as animals speaking with each other and with humans. His Brer Rabbit stories always include one specific rabbit that gets into scrapes because of his brashness, but who always escapes because of his quick wit. The tales are laced with gentle humor.

While aids such as these are helpful, the student should at the same time be encouraged to make educated guesses and to rely as much as possible on the context.[4] And it should be recognized that there is no substitute for substantial exposure in-country to the culture, situations, and frame of mind that produce such language.[5]

The adaptation that is illustrated in Table 7-1 utilizes the two-step process suggested early in this discussion: first, a regularizing of spelling, then a standardizing of the dialect.

Table 7-1   Adaptations of "Brer Rabbit and the Little Girl"

Original[1]

"One time, after Brer Rabbit done bin trompin' roun' huntin' up some sallid fer ter make out he dinner wid, he fine hisse'f in de neighborhoods er Mr. Man house, en he pass 'long twel he come ter de gyardin-gate, en nigh de gyardin-gate he see Little Gal playin' roun' in de san'. / W'en Brer Rabbit look 'twix de gyardin-palin's en see de colluds, en de sparrer-grass, en de yuther gyardin truck growin' dar, hit make he mouf water. Den he take en walk up ter de Little Gal, Brer Rabbit did, en pull he roach, en bow, en scrape he foot, en talk mighty nice en slick.

" 'Howdy, Little Gal,' sez Brer Rabbit, sezee; 'how you come on?' sezee.

"Den de Little Gal, she 'spon' howdy, she did, en she asks Brer Rabbit how he come on, en Brer Rabbit, he 'low he mighty po'ly, en den he ax ef dis de Little Gal w'at 'er pa live up dar in de big w'ite house, w'ich de Little Gal, she up'n say 'twer'. Brer Rabbit, he say he mighty glad, kaze he des bin up dar fer to see 'er pa, en he say dat 'er pa, he sont 'im out dar fer ter tell de Little Gal dat she mus' open de gyardin-gate so Brer Rabbit kin go in en git some truck. Den de Little Gal, she jump roun', she did, en she open de gate, en wid dat, Brer Rabbit, he hop in, he did, en got 'im a mess er greens, en hop out ag'in, en w'en he gwine off he make a bow, he did, en tell de Little Gal dat he much 'blige', en den he put out fer home."

Adaptation 1:
Spelling regularized

A. "One time, after Brother Rabbit done been tramping around hunting up some salad for to make out he dinner with, he find himself in the neighborhoods of Mr. Man house, and he pass along till he come to the garden gate, and nigh the garden gate he see Little Gal playing round in the sand."

B. " 'Howdy, Little Gal,' says Brother Rabbit, says he; 'how you come on?' says he.

"Then the Little Gal, she responds howdy, she did, and she asks Brother Rabbit how he come on, and Brother Rabbit, he allow he mighty poorly, and then he asks if this the Little Gal what her pa live up there in the big white house, which the Little Gal, she up and say it were."

C. "Then the Little Gal, she jump round, she did, and she open the gate, and with that, Brother Rabbit, he hop in, he did, and got him a mess of greens, and hop out again, and when he going off he make a bow, he did, and tell the Little Gal that he much oblige, and then he put out for home."

[1] In Harris 1955, p. 126.

Adaptation 2:
Full regularization

"One time, Brother Rabbit had been tramping about trying to find some greens so that he could make a salad for lunch. Suddenly he found himself in the vicinity of Mr. Man's house. He continued along until he came to the garden gate, and near the gate he saw a little girl playing in the sand."

"Hello, little girl," said Brother Rabbit; "how are you doing?"

"Then the little girl said hello, in return and asked Brother Rabbit how he was doing. Brother Rabbit replied that he wasn't doing very well. Then he asked if she were the little girl whose father lived nearby in the big white house, and she answered that she was."

"Then the little girl hurried right over and opened the gate. At that, Brother Rabbit hopped right in, got himself a bunch of greens, and hopped out again. As he was leaving, he bowed and thanked the little girl. Then he set out for home."

Notice that this is done with excerpts and not with the entire selection, in order to encourage students to extrapolate meaning on their own between the adapted segments.

ADAPTING TO TEMPORAL DIFFERENCES

One final language variation is change which occurs simply through the passage of time. Bolinger (1975) views this inevitable change in relation to the stabilizing forces of language:

> Every living language is in a state of dynamic equilibrium. Infinitesimal changes occur in every act of speech, and mostly make no impression. . . . Now and then a scintillation is captured and held. We hear a novel expression and like it. It is adaptive—fits a style or names a new object or expresses an idea succinctly. Others take it up and it "becomes part of the language." The equilibrium is temporarily upset but reestablishes itself quickly. The new expression, like an invading predator, marks out its territory, and the older inhabitants defend what is left of theirs.
>
> The vast open-endedness of language that results from multiple reinvestment is what makes it both systematic and receptive to change. The parts are intricately interwoven, and this maintains the fabric; but they are also infinitely recombinable, and this makes for gradual, nondestructive variation. [P. 17.]

Those who are literate have a reasonably high tolerance for written material in their native language that is somewhat antiquated, whereas a slightly archaic text trips up most second-language learners rather badly. We begin to appreciate their difficulty when we attempt to cope with this spell from an Old English text:

> Hal wes þu, folde, fira modor,
> beo þu growende on godes faeþ me,
> fodre gefylled firum to nytte. . . .

(Hale be thou, earth, mother of men,
be thou with growing things in God's embrace,
filled with food for the good of men. . . .)
                    ["Æcerbot," in Baugh 1948, p. 41.]

or even a Middle English text:

A gentil Maunciple was ther of a temple,
Of which achatours mighte take exemple
For to be wyse in bying of vitaille
For whether that he payde, or took by taille,
Algate he wayted so in his achat,
That he was ay biforn and in good stat.
                    [Chaucer in Donaldson 1975, ll. 567-574.]

On the other hand, a seventeenth century piece such as this one by Donne we can readily comprehend. But not so the nonnative speaker:

17. Meditation. Perchance hee for whom this Bell tolls, may be so ill, as that he knowes not it tolls for him; And perchance I may thinke my selfe so much better than I am, as that they who are about mee, and see my state, may have caused it to toll for mee, and I know not that. . . . [In Gardner and Healy 1967, p. 100.]

Even after their long period of classroom incubation, during which time they have been carefully taught their new language and nourished on simplified, graded texts, second-language learners inevitably find the transition to unsimplified prose a painfully difficult one. While not many will encounter John Donne, quite a number will ultimately encounter language contemporary with Donne—Shakespeare or the Bible—as well as the more manageable but often unfamiliar prose and poetry of the eighteenth and nineteenth centuries. Without assistance of some kind, the nonnative speaker may find Carlyle, Huxley, Hazlitt, Jefferson, Franklin, Emerson too big a step to take.

Again, it would be possible simply to avoid teaching such difficult prose in advanced classes, or to present it in updated versions. But we reject this solution as crippling to students who want or need information and experience in the full range of English literature. With guidance, almost any student can understand and appreciate the superior quality of literature produced by the greatest writers in the English language. Avoidance is a self-defeating policy when applied across the board.

The most obvious difficulties in the selection by Donne are archaic words and spelling, but even more challenging are the long, complex, heavily embedded sentences with their often unfamiliar syntax. Allusions and figurative language constitute additional stumbling blocks.

Occasionally, modern paraphrases are available for reference; but one limitation with this remedy is the temptation to always use the paraphrase as a substitute or as a crutch. An alternate approach in an advanced reading class would be for the teacher to begin with contemporary material, then move backwards in time gradually: first looking at easily comprehended short stories, novels, and familiar essays, then ultimately moving to more scholarly or more difficult literary selections. Class discussion is an important adjunct. The introductory "prevision" might include not only what to look for but also information on the subject at hand, the period, and author, as well as key phrases, imagery, etc. Longer selections could be managed a part at a time through intensive discussions that would prepare for subsequent reading.

It is our recommendation that in addition to class discussion, the language teacher should adapt occasional segments of particularly difficult selections.[6] Table 7-2 illustrates three possible forms of adaptation, but of course only one form would be used at any one time; and a smaller ratio of adapted lines would be prepared. These adapted segments provide the student with assistance he can draw upon outside class but also force him to grapple with unadapted texts on his own. This procedure reflects our view that the aim should be to read the original text, not only because modern paraphrases are seldom available but also because of the literary merits of the original.

In addition to the possibility of editing, suggested earlier in the chapter, one might simply update the spelling, punctuation, and capitalization. The three forms of adaptation illustrated in Table 7-2 are (1) a version with modernized

Table 7-2   Adaptations of Donne's "Meditation"

Original[1]

17. Meditation. Perchance hee for whom this Bell tolls, may be so ill, as that he knowes not it tolls for him. And perchance I may thinke my selfe so much better than I am, as that they who are about mee, and see my state, may have caused it to toll for mee, and I know not that.

The Church is Catholike, universall, so are all her Actions; All that she does, belongs to all. When she baptizes a child, that action concernes mee; for that child is thereby connected to that Head which is my Head too, and engraffed into that body, whereof I am a member. And when she buries a Man, that action concernes me:

All mankinde is of one Author, and is one volume; when one Man dies, one Chapter is not torne out of the booke, but translated into a better language; and every Chapter must be so translated; God emploies several translators; some peeces are translated by age, some by sicknesse, some by warre, some by justice; but Gods hand is in every translation and his hand shall binde up all our scattered leaves againe, for that Librarie where every booke shall lie open to one another: As therefore the Bell that rings to a Sermon, calls not upon the Preacher onely, but upon the Congregation to come; so this Bell calls us all: but how much more mee, who am brought so neere the doore by this sicknesse. . . .

If we understand aright the dignitie of this Bell that tolls for our evening prayer, wee would bee glad to make it ours, by rising early, in that application that it might bee ours, as wel as his, whose indeed it is. The Bell doth toll for him that thinkes it doth; and though it intermit againe, yet from that minute, that that occasion wrought upon him, hee is united to God. Who casts not up his Eie to the Sunne when it rises? but who takes off his Eie from a Comet when that breakes out? Who bends not his eare to any bell, which upon any occasion rings? but who can remove it from that bell, which is passing a peece of himselfe out of this world? No man is an Iland, intire of it selfe; every man is a peece of the Continent, a part of the maine; if a Clod bee washed away by the Sea, Europe is the lesse, as well as if a Promontorie were as well as if a Mannor of thy friends or of thine owne were; any mans death diminishes me, because I am involved in Mankinde; And therefore never send to know for whom the bell tolls; It tolls for thee. . . .

Table 7-2 (continued)

Adaptation 1: Modernization with minimal alteration	*Adaptation 2: Modernized paraphrase with figurative expressions removed*	*Adaptation 3: Simplification*
A. Perhaps he for whom this bell is tolling is so ill he does not know it is tolling for him. Or perhaps I think my health is better than it actually is, but those around me seeing my condition have caused it to be tolled for me, without my knowing it.	[A church bell is being rung on behalf of someone dead or dying.] Perhaps he is so ill he does not know the bell is ringing for him. Or is it ringing for me without my knowing it? Perhaps my health is worse than I think. And maybe those around me, who can see my condition, are having it rung for me.	Someone is ringing a church bell; he thinks that will help a sick or dead person. But maybe this person is very sick and doesn't know it is for him. Or maybe the bell is ringing for me, and I do not know it. Perhaps people see that my health is bad, when I think it is good. Are they ringing the bell for me?
B. All mankind is from one author and in one volume. When a man dies, a chapter is not torn from the book; instead it is translated into a better language. And every chapter must be similarly translated. Some portions are translated by age, some by sickness. . . .	God created all men; therefore there is a common bond among them. When a man dies, he is not separated from his fellow men; he simply enters a superior kind of existence. Moreover, every individual must go through this same transition. God uses various means to bring this transition about. Old age is one means, sickness another. . . .	God made all people. So people think and feel like each other. After a person dies, he lives again in a better place. All people go there when they die. So everyone will be together again. Some people die because they are very old. Other people die because they are very sick. . . .

C. No man is an island, complete in and of itself. Every man is part of a continent, part of the mainland. If a clod is washed away by the sea, Europe is diminished just as if an entire promontory were inundated.... Similarly, any man's death diminishes me, because I am part of mankind. Therefore, never inquire who the bell is tolling for. It is tolling for you.

No man is entirely independent of others. He is an integral part of all mankind. The loss of a single individual is as significant as the loss of an entire city.... When a man dies, it is as though part of me also passed away, so much am I part of all mankind. Consequently, when you hear a church bell ringing, never ask who it is being rung for. Since you too are part of mankind, it is ringing for you.

Every person depends on other people, and every person is part of mankind.[2] Each person is important. So, when one dies, it is like losing many people—even a city of people.... When a person dies, it is like losing part of myself—an eye or an arm. Sometime you will hear a church bell. It will be ringing for someone, but do not ask his name. You are part of mankind, so it will be ringing for you.

[1]In Gardner and Healy 1967, pp. 100-101.
[2]Mankind: everyone who has ever lived, everyone who is now living, and everyone who will live.

spelling, but close to the original syntax and vocabulary; (2) a modernized paraphrase which departs from the original syntax and figurative language; and (3) a greatly simplified version with controlled vocabulary and syntax—normally a maximum of one embedded clause per sentence, and virtual elimination of nominalizations, modals, perfect tenses, and conditionals. Understandably, there is a progressive loss of force and artistry as we move from the original to the simplification. The simplified version provides only a skeleton of the original semantic content; rhetorical, stylistic, and esthetic qualities have been sacrificed for the literal meaning of the passage. Especially when dealing with works of literature, it should be remembered that the meaning and impact of a selection rely not only on the message, or surface meaning, but also on such varied components as word selection and arrangement, rhetorical-stylistic features, figurative and symbolic language, and even the very sounds and rhythm of the author's prose—not to mention his undergirding concepts and values. Paraphrase and simplification, then, are *temporary* aids to a fuller understanding and appreciation of the unadapted version.

In this chapter we have considered how to cope with speech variety that we normally regard as involuntary. We have concluded that, in general, only a passive awareness of such differences is needed. As teachers, the rules of thumb are simple: help the student avoid usage that for him or her would be inappropriate; and when these differences threaten to interfere with comprehension, provide adaptation that will lead to an understanding of the original.

NOTES

1. Activists among those who wish to eradicate "sexist" linguistic items will claim that the language of textbooks should be purged of any terms or features that mark sex, especially those which suggest male preference or dominance. We feel that a language textbook should reflect existing usage and not what someone thinks ought to prevail. It has been just a

few years since a battle raged between prescriptive and descriptive grammarians over rationalized prestige forms of language, i.e., "good grammar" and "bad grammar." Feminists are advocating that terms such as *chairperson, garbage collector, police officer,* and *mail deliverer* be used in place of *chairman, garbage man, policeman, mailman,* etc. If these gain currency, they will need to be introduced. Until then, we feel students will be better served with instruction that incorporates lexical items used by the majority of native speakers. Obviously, serious language students will also be interested in important trends as well as organized efforts to effect change.

2. Normally, contrasts in British-American speech or grammatical usage are very minor and reflect preference rather than strict patterns of usage. In the present example, usage differs rather significantly, to an extent that adjustment for dialect seems desirable. There is no particular benefit, generally, in calling attention to differences in British and American speech, unless not knowing seems to bother students. The labels in the sample are for the reader's benefit.

3. One recommended device to elicit question forms is the use of indirect questions as suggested in Chapter 1. The teacher addresses two students: "Paul, ask Ann how many cars Mr. Benning has." After Paul does this, Ann may answer without a specific prompt, but if not, the teacher says, "Answer Paul, Ann."

4. Cf. Twaddell 1973, pp. 61-78.

5. It was undoubtedly this awareness that prompted Donald J. Lloyd and Harry Warfel to write their convincing "Thirty Years to a More Powerful Vocabulary."

6. For particularly apt students, paraphrase writing in modern idiom could be assigned.

CHAPTER 8
SIMPLIFICATION

In discussing language variety, we have considered the need to communicate in appropriate language codes and to avoid picking up unsuitable forms. We have seen, too, that the teacher can assist student comprehension of unusual regional, social, and archaic language by standardizing written selections. In this further chapter on language variety, we will discuss ways in which even standard speech or writing can be adapted to meet the needs of certain groups. For instance, children learning a second or foreign language often find the lexis and syntax of adults more than they can cope with. And the technical language of professional journals tends to elude the grasp of adults whose reading has been limited to graded readers with controlled vocabulary and structures. Judicious simplification can provide significant assistance in such cases.

ADAPTING MATERIAL FOR CHILDREN

Assuming a variety of reading materials for the children one is teaching, an obvious initial step is to evaluate their suitability for readers at this age level. In addition to assessing linguistic difficulty, we need to consider their appeal and appropriateness. In her impressive work on children's books, Arbuthnot (1957) returns again and again to the importance of interest: " . . . a book is a good book for children only when they enjoy it; a book is a poor book for children, even when adults rate it a classic, if children are unable to read it or are bored by its content" (p. 2). She offers her opinion on what makes a book interesting to children:

> In general, children like stories with an *adequate theme,* strong enough to generate and support a *lively* plot. They appreciate memorable characters and distinctive style. [P. 16. Arbuthnot's italics.]

> Aesthetic satisfaction comes to the small child as well as to the adult. . . . [P. 11.]

Phyllis and Mark Dintenfass (1967) recommend stories that are short, that have a point and maintain interest while avoiding complex ideas (p. 5). Authorities tend to agree that violence, cruelty, sexual acts, and coarse language are inappropriate in stories for children; and that tales with sad endings or many double meanings fail to interest most children.[1]

Besides reading and subjectively evaluating children's stories ourselves, we can determine interest—as Carroll (1967) does—by soliciting student reactions and then keeping a score sheet on each book (pp. 34-40). He also gets students' opinions on whether the book is too easy, too difficult, or about right for their grade.

A still more exact measure of level of difficulty can be obtained by using the cloze procedure (see Table 8-1). A representative selection or two is extracted from the story or book. One avoids using introductory or concluding portions and segments containing many proper nouns or numbers. The extract should make good sense even when read out of context. The first sentence or two is left intact. Then every seventh word is deleted throughout the balance of the excerpt, for a total of at least 25 to 30 words. Students are requested to read through the passage to get an overview of the meaning, and then fill in the blanks. An easy and reliable scoring procedure for this purpose is to give credit for only the exact word. If one obtains a measure on a couple of stories that the class has been able to read with little difficulty, he can then use the class average on these as a yardstick to compare scores on other stories with.

Table 8-1   Using the cloze procedure to evaluate level of difficulty*

Cloze Samples

Directions (for teacher to read aloud): Do not write anything in the blanks yet. First, read the whole story. Then begin again and write one word in each blank. Contractions like "she's" or "won't" are just one word. Put in words that sound right. Every blank should have a word in it; no blank should have more than one word. When you finish, read the story again. Make sure your words sound right in the blanks.

Story 1:

Sam and Andy have three meals a day: breakfast, lunch, and dinner. They have breakfast at home. On _____ (1) they have lunch at school, but _____ (2) weekends they have lunch at home _____ (3) their parents. They always eat dinner _____ (4) home.

Dinner is the big meal _____ (5) the day. Mr. Scott comes home _____ (6) work at five, and Mrs. Scott _____ (7) dinner at six. They usually start _____ (8) soup. Then they have meat, potatoes, _____ (9) salad.

After dinner they have dessert. _____ (10) Scott doesn't like desserts, but Mrs. _____ (11) and the children do. Their favorite _____ (12) are cake and ice cream.

Teacher key
1. weekdays
2. on
3. with
4. at
5. of
6. from
7. serves
8. with
9. and
10. Mr.
11. Scott
12. desserts

Story 2:

Kim helped her mother last weekend. This is what she did. She did the housework. She did _____ (13) dishes. She made the beds. She _____ (14) the meals. She got breakfast, lunch, _____ (15) dinner. She made dessert. She made _____ (16) pie and a cake.

Mrs. Lee _____ (17) have to do any house work last _____ (18). She went shopping instead.

Tek didn't _____ (19) at the supermarket last weekend. He _____ (20) home and helped his father. He _____ (21) do the house-

13. the
14. got
15. and
16. a
17. didn't
18. weekend
19. work
20. stayed
21. didn't

Source: Slager 1972, pp. 166, 240.

Table 8-1 (continued)

	Teacher key
work. This is what _____ (22) did. He	22. he
cleaned the garage. He _____ (23) the car.	23. washed
He worked at home _____ (24) day.	24. all
Mr. Lee didn't go shopping. _____ (25)	25. He
doesn't like to go shopping. He stayed home and	
worked with Tek.	

In addition, there are formulas that have been developed by reading specialists, e.g., the Flesch formula, Fry formula, Dale-Chall formula, and the Spache formula. The Flesch and Fry formulas cover the entire range of grades from elementary school through high school. The more complicated Spache and Dale-Chall formulas are somewhat restricted in scope: the Spache readability formula being most applicable from kindergarten through third grade, and the Dale-Chall from the third or fourth grade through the early college years (grades 4-14). The latter two formulas concentrate on sentence length and vocabulary levels. Reading specialists Floyd Sucher and Ruel Allred indicate that if proper nouns are simply ignored when applying the Fry Readability Graph, one can obtain essentially the same results as those from the more complex, longer formulas. The Fry readability formula is reproduced as an appendix to this volume. The Spache formula can be found in George D. Spache's *Good Reading for Poor Readers* (Champaign, Illinois: Garrard Publishing Company 1974). The advantages in using one of these readability formulas are that estimates of specific grade levels can be arrived at and evaluations can be made without infringing on class time.

After available reading materials have been evaluated for interest and suitability, it may be found that additional readings are needed. Since identifying and acquiring additional appropriate texts can be expensive and time-consuming, the teacher may want to enlarge his offering by producing supplementary materials of his own. Finocchiaro (1969) describes how even young school children can contribute to such an effort. She suggests having them engage in some interesting experience such as a field trip (or possibly a movie or story read aloud in class). Following an informal discussion of the experience, the teacher can ask questions which the students respond to. The responses are written in narrative form on the board, with needed transitions supplied (pp. 146-148). These could be copied into student notebooks or transferred by the teacher to booklets for circulation. Students able to write could tap community resources individually and write up stories ranging from local legends or folk stories to "how to" accounts of vanishing crafts and activities. These would be edited and revised, then transferred to booklets which would serve as class readers.

From time to time, particularly overseas, it happens that interesting reading material is available but that the level is too advanced for most class members. If easier books cannot readily be obtained, the teacher may choose to simplify some stories. In doing so, she will need to maintain (or introduce) adequate redundancy, reduce clause length and embedding, and deal with lexical difficulties such as abstractions, figurative language, and low-frequency items. Like Stevick (1971, p. 64), we feel that good adaptation and simplification is an art rather than a mechanical process, but that some helpful guidelines can be formulated.

An initial caution is to avoid mere abridgment or condensation in the name of simplification. While overseas, we observed some well-intentioned "simplification" which simply compressed into shorter sentences the ideas expressed in longer ones. Ironically, this often tends to make the material more difficult to read than the original. The key here is to increase rather than decrease redundancy. "Redundancy" in this context does not, of course, refer to "superfluous repetition" but, as Wonderly (1968) indicates, to "the kind of redundancy that is generally characteristic of all language and without which normal communication would be difficult if not impossible" (P. 169.]

He illustrates grammatical and lexical redundancy: In "he sings," for example, the inflectional ending on the verb is redundant since the third person singular has already been indicated by the subject. "This kind of redundancy," says

Wonderly, "is essentially a repetition of information." It facilitates communication by helping us to anticipate what is to follow or to confirm what we have already heard—but perhaps haven't heard clearly. A lexical example of redundancy is the sentence *The ducks _____ed at the top of their voices,* where *quack* is virtually the only appropriate word that can be inserted in the context of *duck* and *voice* (ibid.). Partial lexical redundancy, says Wonderly, is illustrated in a sentence such as "He sings beautifully" where semantic context makes an adverb such as *mathematically* unlikely and a noun such as *elephant* virtually impossible, despite the fact that we could have the sentence *He sings tenor.* Most of us have also noted orthographic redundancy as well: *Rxally, is xvxry kxy on thx typxwritxr, nxcxssary?*

Natural redundancy in language helps us communicate not only in a noisy setting but also in written contexts:

> ... the redundancies in written material help the reader to understand words and grammatical relationships that he does not know, or knows imperfectly, by enabling him to "fill in the blanks" from information present elsewhere in the context. This means that, for any level of readership, the skillful writer or translator anticipates his readers' difficulties and builds in extra redundancy at points where the going is rough and the communication load is in danger of getting above the horizon of difficulty of the intended readers. The particular amount of redundancy in a given passage will depend, then, on the level of the readers and the difficulty of the material. [Ibid., p. 170.]

> Another way of stating the function of redundancy is to say that it prevents overloading.... Information presented in too concentrated a form (too much new information per minute, per clause, or per page) places the materials beyond the reader's horizon of difficulty and thus out of his reach. By increasing the overall redundancy, the information content is presented in less concentrated form, or at a slower rate per minute or per page, thus enabling the reader to assimilate it. [Ibid., p. 171.]

There are various ways in which needed redundancy can be achieved. One means is through repetition of key words or phrases and maintaining nouns that might otherwise be pronominalized. Observe these features in the following:

Jack be nimble, / Jack be quick, / and Jack jump over the candlestick.

Humpty Dumpty sat on a wall, / Humpty Dumpty had a great fall; / All the King's horses and all the King's men / couldn't put Humpty together again.

This is the house that Jack built.
This is the malt / That lay in the house that Jack built.
This is the rat, / That ate the malt / That lay in the house that Jack built.

> . . . "Will you see any whales?" asked Barbara.
> "Of course not!" said Bill. "Whales live near the South Pole, silly, and Uncle William isn't going there."
> "I might easily see whales, Bill," said Uncle William.
> [Wolff and Spencer 1966, p. 55.]

I remember the smell of sea and seaweed, wet flesh, wet hair, wet bathing-dresses, the warm smell as of a rabbity field after rain, the smell of pop and splashed sunshades and toffee, the stable-and-straw smell of hot, tossed, tumbled, dug and trodden sand. . . . [Dylan Thomas 1954, pp. 32-33.]

He came, he saw, he conquered.

. . . we cannot dedicate—we cannot consecrate—we cannot hallow—this ground.

. . . of the people, by the people, for the people . . .

Another means is to reduce embedding:

She knows when he's leaving *or* She knows he's leaving at 6:15.	He's leaving at 6:15. And she knows it.
Whoever it was you promised to meet called an hour ago to find out where you were.	A girl called you an hour ago. You had promised to meet her. She wondered where you were.

For those who might want to eliminate all embedding, the final sentence (*She wondered . . .*) might be recast as *She asked a question: "Where is he?"* Note the cost, however, of linguistic realism.

The teacher can also increase needed redundancy by reducing nominalizations:

Their decision regarding our request was very disappointing.	We requested permission to leave a week early. They decided we couldn't. That disappointed us very much.

In brief, needed redundancy can be provided by unobtrusive repetition of information. This happens constantly in conversation. Someone asks if we're going to a game. Smiling and nodding our heads in the affirmative, we reply, "Yep, I wouldn't miss it. I'll be there all right. You can count on it." Including the two nonverbal clues, we have said *yes* at least six times in response.

Consider the numerous forms of redundancy in this single sentence: *In her art class this semester, Ann paints at least two portraits a week of anyone she wants to.*

art class / paints / portraits
her / Ann / she
portraits / anyone

two / portraits   *and*   this / semester
Ann / paints   *and*   she / wants

Redundancy of the latter variety helps us anticipate what is to follow. John Oller refers to this as "expectancy grammar." Wonderly points out that metaphorical expressions are troublesome because they violate the reader's expectancy. In the sentence *He decided to manicure his . . .* , there is high expectation of *fingernails* as the following word. "But suppose," says Wonderly,

> the same reader encounters Gibson Winter's metaphorical expression *to . . . manicure his private feelings.* Since feelings, whether private or public, are not normally

manicured, the last two words of the expression are highly unpredictable and unexpected—so much so that an inexperienced reader might reject them as unbelievable even if he did recognize them. For Winter's intended audience the expression is an effective use of metaphor; for the new reader it would be too unpredictable for good readability. [Pp. 171-172.]

In addition to redundancy, the simplifier of reading selections is obliged to give attention to vocabulary. An obvious concern is to avoid low-frequency words. Those interested in carefully controlled vocabulary will need to consult a recognized frequency list.[2] Each list has its special advantages and limitations. A special advantage of Michael West's list is that it indicates the frequency of each meaning of a given word; for example, *table* is a high frequency word when used to mean an item of furniture but rather low frequency when used to mean a chart or a geographical formation, or when used as a verb in parliamentary procedure. Whichever list is used, the purpose, of course, is to select easier, more common words. Another way of coping with difficult but essential words is to in effect define them in an adjoining sentence. For example, in a fable that we will look at shortly, the focus is on a thirsty crow. If we would like the student to become familiar with *thirsty* but see no need for his learning the word *crow*, we could begin:

Once there was a (black)bird. He wanted a drink of water. But there was no water anywhere. The blackbird was very thirsty.

Notice, too, that in renaming the bird we utilize the technique of appropriating a transparent word. Thus a *ferocious* lion could become a *man-eating* lion; *barren* could become *childless; crotched, V-shaped; bellicose, warlike; arduous toil, back-breaking work; sin, wrong-doing; naive, childlike,* etc. Notice, too, that even these transparent words or expressions can be made still more obvious (as in the case of nominalizations) by transforming them into clauses. Thus we have *barren* → *childless* → *(She) had no children.*

As suggested earlier, figurative language, euphemisms, and the like often need equating with a more direct expression in order to be understood:

unvarnished truth	complete truth
father was taken from us	father died
bread and butter letter	letter expressing thanks for hospitality
hard pill to swallow	difficult to accept
puppet leaders	leaders who are controlled by others
intellectually they were all blank cartridges	none of them were intelligent
he jigsawed between the players	he ran back and forth (in and out) between the players
How beautiful upon the mountains are the feet of him that bringeth good tidings. . . .	How honored is the herald of good news! *or* People love the person who brings good news.
TV is a kind of intellectual thumbsucking.	There is no intellectual nourishment in watching television.

The same is true of abstractions. Sometimes the word can in effect be defined in context. Sometimes a narrative or dramatic situation can illustrate the abstraction, as it does the moral that concludes the Aesop fable about the wise crow: "Necessity is the mother of invention." (See the simplification of the fable later in this chapter.) And sometimes a rather general word can be made more concrete. A few examples follow:

truth   He told the truth: When his mother asked him if he had broken the glass, he said, "Yes, I did."

happiness   School was over at last. It was a beautiful sunny day but not too hot. He smiled as he ate a piece of chocolate cake on his way to the swimming pool. Now he knew what happiness meant: no school, warm days, cake, and swimming.

an animal went into the store   His little collie dog ran quickly into Macy's cool department store.

From vocabulary, we now move to syntax as a means of simplifying language. Generally speaking, there is a positive correlation between sentence length and grammatical complexity. A simple alternative to sentence length as a measure of complexity or difficulty is clause length. But neither the sentence nor the clause is the best indicator of syntactic complexity. As indicated in the redundancy discussion, a long sentence can be semantically simple and a short sentence can be quite complex and difficult. This is because a long sentence can consist of a series of simple independent clauses joined by coordinating conjunctions such as *and*; and the same sentence can be rewritten as a series of shorter sentences by changing only the punctuation. There is effectively no difference between the level of difficulty of this single long sentence and the shorter ones. On the other hand, dependent clauses cannot be separated from the rest of the sentence they occur in merely by repunctuating.

Kellogg W. Hunt (1965) has defined what he terms a T-unit as an independent clause plus any associated dependent clause(s). This is a kind of minimal independent sentence. And the mean length of T-units turns out to be the most reliable index of syntactic difficulty (pp. 300-309).

Observe in the following passage from Sherwood Anderson's "I'm A Fool" that eight clauses consisting of seven T-units are written in only two sentences:

> And I was with that girl and she wasn't saying much, and I wasn't saying much either. . . . you want that girl to be your wife, and you want nice things around her like flowers and swell clothes, and you want her to have the kids you're going to have, and you want good music played and no rag time. [1923, p. 15.]

For stylistic reasons, Ernest Hemingway separates the six clauses in the following excerpt from "The Killers" into five sentences corresponding precisely with five T-units. The essential stylistic difference is Anderson's use of the coordinating conjunction *and* (six times) at the beginning of his T-units.

> Outside it was getting dark. The streetlight came on outside the window. The two men at the counter read the

menu. From the other end of the counter Nick Adams watched them. He had been talking to George when they came in. [1927, p. 78.]

The point is, of course, that both excerpts are easy to read, despite major differences in sentence length: The average sentence length in the first example is 29.5 words; the average in the second is 8.4 words. But T-unit length is virtually identical—8.43 per T-unit in the Anderson selection, compared with 8.40 in Hemingway.

In very short utterances the T-unit usually corresponds to a sentence. We can therefore seriously consider the recommendations of specialists in children's literature for optimum length of sentences. The Dintenfasses recommend a five- or six-word average, with a seven- or eight-word maximum.

As we have indicated earlier, simplified reading selections should be not only short but also relatively unimbedded. Here are some examples of how to eliminate difficult constructions ranging from subordinate clauses, including conditionals, to infinitives and modals:

Unsimplified	*Simplified*
The milk in this pail will provide me with cream, which I will make into butter. (Aesop)	I will take the cream from this milk. And I will make butter from the cream.
When the moon rose over the mountains, he slipped out of his tent.	The moon rose over the mountains. Then he stepped quietly out of his tent.
I know he doesn't like me.	He doesn't like me. I know it. *or* I know this.
If you ask him politely to accompany you, he'll do so.	Say to him, "Please come with me." And he will.
I'm sure she'd like to eat before leaving.	She leaves soon. She wants some food now; I'm sure of it.
He's had ample time; he should easily have arrived home by now.	The trip to his home takes fifteen minutes. He left at noon, and it's 12:30 now. He's home; I'm sure.

For the good of the neighbor- hood you ought to sell that noisy dog.	That dog barks all day. Sell him; why don't you. You and your neighbors will be happier.

Still another device for simplifying reading matter is editing. Complex and difficult ideas can be eliminated if they are not essential to the story. Occasionally, even nonessential descriptive phrases can be omitted, though for adults much of a story's charm stems from such description. Observe the editing in this introduction to a Turkish folk tale called "The Turban" (in Juda 1963, p. 5).

Unsimplified	*Edited*
He stood on the shady steps of the general store, hands in pockets, swaying like a tree bent by the wind, peering down at his reflection in the muddy pool.	Old Nasreddin stood in front of the store. His hands were in his pockets. There was some dirty water on the ground, and Nasreddin saw himself in the water.

Note that despite the elimination of an eight-word phrase, the adapted version is almost exactly the same length as the original.

We are now prepared to simplify a brief story by providing adequate redundancy, lexical and syntactic adjustment, and if necessary some editing.

Unsimplified	*Simplified*
The Crow and the Pitcher	The Blackbird and the Bottle of Water
A thirsty Crow found a Pitcher with some water in it, but so little was there that, try as she might, she could not reach it with her beak, and it seemed as though she would die of thirst within sight of the remedy. At last she hit upon a clever plan. She began dropping pebbles into the Pitcher, and with each pebble the water rose a little higher until at	Once there was a blackbird. She wanted a drink of water. But there was no water anywhere. The blackbird was very thirsty. At last she found a bottle. There was water in the bottle. It was half full of water. But her neck was very short, and she could not put her head inside the bottle. So she could not drink the water. "There is water

last it reached the brim, and the knowing bird was enabled to quench her thirst.

"Necessity is the mother of invention."

in the bottle, but I will die," she said.

Then she thought of something. Nearby were many small stones. She picked up a little stone, and she put it in the bottle. Then she put another stone in the bottle, and another. Now the water was higher in the bottle. She put in another stone and another.

At last the water was at the top. The clever blackbird drank the water.

Redundancy is effected in a variety of ways, for example by taking a phrase such as *with some water in it* and expanding it into a sentence. Lexical assistance is provided by clarifying *thirsty,* using the transparent *blackbird* for *crow,* substituting the more common *bottle* for *pitcher,* and eliminating relatively difficult words such as *reach, beak, thirst, sight, remedy, plan, drop, pebble, rise, brim, enable, quench,* and *necessity.* Also avoided are expressions such as *try as she might, hit upon, knowing bird,* and *mother of invention.* Furthermore, clauses are greatly simplified and sentence length dramatically reduced (significant, since the original sentences do not consist primarily of coordinate elements). Also, the passive in the last sentence is eliminated. But because the original is so spare and compact, the only editing is elimination of the abstractly stated moral at the conclusion.

Three other matters deserve attention. One is the use of *short paragraphs* to help maintain interest and to group ideas and events into related clusters. A second is the use of an *illustration* if possible such as that below. Besides helping to spark interest, illustrations provide additional redundancy by reflecting key points being expressed in the story. The third is the occasional use of *expansion,* such as the blackbird's looking everywhere for water, and reference to the shortness of her neck. All three devices are useful adjuncts in simplifying.

In connection with expansion, the Dintenfasses note that some fables, legends, and local tales contain only a skeleton of a story. They suggest that to stimulate interest (and to provide redundancy) it is often advisable to embellish the story with more detail and to add dialog, to use repetition ("young children seem never to be bored by repetition"), and to dramatize it. Following is a brief excerpt from a much longer expanded tale developed by the Dintenfasses (1967, pp. 20-22; see also p. 25):

Original	*Expanded*
Once there were four oxen. Each had a different colour—red, brown, black, and white. One day they ran away from their master's farm and went into the forest.	Once there were four oxen. Each had a different colour. One was red. One was brown. One was black. And one was white. They were very good friends.
	The oxen used to belong to a farmer. Every morning the farmer took them to the field. They had to pull the farmer's plough. They pulled the plough all day. It was hard work. They used to come home very tired.
	"We work very hard," the red ox said one evening after work.
	"Yes," said the brown ox. "We work very hard. My back hurts."
	"But last year," said the black ox, "we used to play and eat grass all day."
	"Last year we were children," said the white ox. "Now we are grown up. We work very hard."

"My back hurts," said the red ox.

"I have an idea," said the brown ox. "We can run away. We can go into the forest. In the forest there is grass. We can eat the grass. We can play all day. We can have fun."

"That is a good idea," said all the oxen together.

The four oxen woke up early the next morning. The farmer was sleeping in his bed. It was very quiet. The oxen found a hole in the fence. They walked through the hole. Then they walked very quickly into the woods.

We have examined in some detail how to simplify stories for children. One brief consideration remains and that is how to modify potentially engaging stories so that "old tales, created by adults for adults" can be used successfully with children. A master at this sort of adaptation was Hans Christian Andersen, whose adaptations are said to be "right" since they "make the stories suitable and understandable for children while maintaining the integrity of the source." Coarse expressions, cruelty, and sexual frankness are dealt with adroitly:

In "East o' the Sun," for instance, adapters have made the strange man, who came each night to the lassie, enter another room or get into another bed. Andersen in "Great Claus and Little Claus" endows the husband of the faithless wife with a special antipathy for "sextons"; so the infidelity motive is amusingly glossed over. Yet neither of these changes interferes in any way with the essential body or style of the story. . . . On the other hand, if the tale requires many changes, it is probably unsuitable for children either in content or style. [Arbuthnot, pp. 313-314.]

In addition to deflections of this sort, unsuitable segments not integral to the story can simply be deleted.

ADAPTING TECHNICAL MATERIAL FOR ADULTS

Language teachers of intermediate to advanced students regularly agonize over the problem of how to bridge the gap between the prose of language texts and that of technical journals and advanced textbooks for native speakers. Certainly, a number of the techniques used in simplifying material for children can be tapped: Building in increased redundancy and adjusting the lexical and syntactic components are understandably critical. To avoid unnecessary repetition of background information presented earlier in the chapter, we shall center our discussion around a sample of technical writing, and let our principles of adaptation grow out of its modification. Let us begin, then, by looking at this excerpt from a technical journal:

> To this end, another experimental task was devised which rendered the two individuals differentially dependent for good outcomes on interperson and interparty exchange. In Morley and Stephenson's experiment the intrusion of interpersonal considerations (in the face-to-face condition) was held to represent an advantage for the "weak" case. The present experiment examines the complementary situation, one in which the intrusion of interparty considerations would be expected to represent an advantage for the "weak" case, because the "strength" was this time based in interpersonal considerations rather than in interparty considerations (as was the case in Morley and Stephenson's experiment). [Short 1974, p. 227.]

Upon reading this, even the native speaker recognizes that a successful simplification would best be carried out by someone with expertise in the subject at hand, providing the individual also understood and could apply principles of adaptation. The language teacher's collaboration with one qualified in the technical subject would obviously be one way to provide the proper combination of expertise. Short of this, we can see what might be accomplished on our own.

We notice immediately a compression and abstractness contributed to by frequent nominalization and repeated use of the passive. While the specialized student could be expected to handle many if not most of the technical terms, he would more than likely still have difficulty with the general vocabulary since such a large number of low-frequency words are used.

In order to encourage independent reading of unsimplified technical material, we recommend the teacher's focusing on simply a few key passages, which might help illuminate much of what is to follow and even some of the preceding paragraphs. From the article just referred to, we have focused on a pivotal paragraph contrasting two experimental approaches.

First of all, we suggest removing some of the difficult nominalization: *The complementary situation* can be rewritten as:

> The writer conducted a new experiment. This new experiment looked at "weak" and "strong" differently.

The phrase *Another experimental task* can be recast into a full sentence: *He conducted a new experiment.* At the same time we can eliminate the passive:

Original	Revision
In Morley and Stephenson's experiment the intrusion of *interpersonal* considerations . . . was held to represent an advantage. . . .	Morley and Stephenson believed that when people discussed problems face-to-face, *interpersonal* emphasis was an advantage. . . .

We see that as people and actions are introduced, the passage seems less abstract.

A third step is to reduce the vocabulary load:

Original	Revision
. . . which rendered the two individuals differentially dependent for good outcomes on interperson and interparty exchange.	Two people tried to solve disagreements with two other people. One person tried to solve the problem by improved personal relationship; the other tried to solve it by reason.

Observe that in eliminating difficult vocabulary we simultaneously introduce a fourth technique: the use of a significant amount of redundancy; three clauses replace the single original clause. Observe how the introduction of people and actions provides almost a visual perception of the ideas being expressed.

In the major example that follows, all of the above techniques are employed. Notice that the increased redundancy in the simplified version inevitably results in a lengthier version. In our example, we quote the entire original pivotal paragraph as well as a portion of the preceding and following paragraphs. However, we produce an adaptation of only the "key" middle paragraph.

Original (unsimplified)	*Adaptation (simplified)*
... To interpret the results [of an experiment by Morley and Stephenson on the effect of medium on negotiation], it is necessary to determine what was the crucial difference between the two sides which was found to interact with medium.	
To this end, another experimental task was devised which rendered the two individuals differentially dependent for good outcomes on interperson and interparty exchange. In Morley and Stephenson's experiment the intrusion of *interpersonal* considerations (in the face-to-face condition) was held to represent an advantage for the "weak" case. The present experiment examines the complementary situation, one in which the intrusion of *interparty* considerations would be expected to represent an advantage for the	The writer of this article wanted to know which difference, in the experiment that Morley and Stephenson carried out, was more important between people who were discussing problems. Therefore, he set up a new experiment. Two people tried to solve disagreements with two other people [problems such as salary discussions]. One person tried to solve the problem mainly by friendship and improved personal relationship (interpersonal exchange); the other tried to solve it mainly by reason and facts (interparty exchange). Morley and Stephenson

"weak" case, because the "strength" was this time based in interpersonal considerations rather than in interparty considerations (as was the case in Morley and Stephenson's experiment).

The critical difference between this experiment and Morley and Stephenson's experiment was in whether or not the subjects' personal views were consonant with the case their role required them to argue. In the earlier experiment, subjects were randomly assigned to roles and their personal feelings were not systematically relevant to the conflict. In the present experiment, personal opinions were made relevant to the conflict which formed the centre of the negotiation. One side always believed in the case he was asked to argue; the other side's personal view was not consistent with his case, indeed in many cases his actual views may have been dissonant with the view the conflict required him to advocate. . . .

believed that when people discussed problems face-to-face, *interpersonal* emphasis was an advantage for those with the weak case—that is, the weak argument. The writer's experiment looked at "weak" and "strong" differently. Here the "strong" position was the one with interpersonal exchange, and not the position based on logic (as in the Morley-Stephenson case). In the new experiment, then, an improved argument (*interparty* intrusion) was an advantage for those with the weak situation—that is, with a presentation based on logic alone.

In implementing instruction involving adapted paragraphs similar to the one just given, we suggest having the student read as much as he can without making reference to the simplified passages. If two or three integrative questions were available for each paragraph (with answers the student could check himself on, at the end of the selection), the student could determine how much of the adaptation he needed to refer to. When reference is needed, it would be well to read through the entire original paragraph and then the entire simplified paragraph in order to view ideas presented in proper perspective. This could be followed if necessary with line-by-line analysis, and where feasible by class discussion.

One further adjunct in simplification of technical material parallels that employed in adapting stories for children, and that is the use of illustrations. Occasionally a chart, graph, or diagram can do wonders in illuminating a complicated concept. In Table 8-2 we attempt to present a visual summary of the concepts expressed in the technical article we have been quoting from.

In concluding this chapter on language variety, we see that, apart from the need to adapt language variety to situation and to adapt difficult archaic or regional language so it can be understood, it is also practical at times to adapt standard varieties of a language—stories too difficult for children, and technical writing too challenging for adults. The purpose of this discussion on simplification has of course been to provide instruction on how to simplify, as well as how to evaluate the simplifying that someone else has done. The key to simplified adaptation, we have seen, consists of providing adequate redundancy and of adjusting both vocabulary and syntax. Occasionally editing, expanding, or illustrating can also ease the learner's task in coping with standard varieties of the new language.

Table 8-2   A visual summary of the article by Short

Experiment One: Morley and Stephenson

Medium	Strong Case (Good argument)	Weak Case (Poor argument)
Face-to-face (personal relationship emphasized)	—	+*
Telephone (logic emphasized)	+	—

*The WEAK *case* is stronger where there is an emphasis on personal relationships (interpersonal focus).

Experiment Two: Short

Medium	Strong Position (Interpersonal approach) Personal relationship	Weak Position (Interparty approach) Facts & reasoning
Face-to-face (personal relation- ship emphasized)	+	—
Telephone (logic emphasized)	—	+*

*The WEAK *position* is stronger where the situation focuses on facts and logic (interparty focus).

NOTES

1. There are exceptions where truly great literature is involved, with quite different messages communicated to children and adults: Cervantes, *Don Quixote*; Swift, *Gulliver's Travels*; Mark Twain, *Huckleberry Finn*; Lewis Carroll, *Alice in Wonderland*; etc.

2. Such as the 3,000 word Dale List (Edgar Dale 1948, pp. 45-54), the Thorndike-Lorge list (E. L. Thorndike and I. Lorge, *The Teacher's Word Book of 30,000 Words* 1944), West's list (Michael West, *A General Service List of English Words* 1953), or the more recent work by Edgar Dale and Joseph O'Rourke (*The Living Word Vocabulary* 1976).

SECTION FOUR

ADMINISTRATIVE AND PEDAGOGICAL CONCERNS

CHAPTER 9

OBJECTIVES, MOTIVATION, AND NATIVE-SPEAKER TEXTS

This final chapter provides an opportunity to consider several pedagogical, administrative, and organizational matters that concern language education and in particular the adjustments that are required to adapt materials and curricula to needs they perhaps were not intended for.

ADAPTING TO VARIED EDUCATIONAL OBJECTIVES

Educational objectives have changed in the past, and they will certainly change in the future. No one in our day would seriously justify the inclusion of Latin in an educational program as an exercise in mental discipline carried out to improve a student's powers of logical analysis. We have likewise largely abandoned the belief that the maximum achievement that can be expected in foreign language instruction in the United States is the ability to decode written materials with the help of a dictionary and a grammar if necessary. Nevertheless, the reading-translation objective continues in certain teaching situations for students who use English as a library language, as an educational tool to provide access to the rich store of texts in written English. Such students may never need to interpret a lecture, write a paper, or communicate face-to-face with an English speaker, but will still need to be familiar with the written form of the language in order to fulfill their educational objectives.

How different from the training needs of hotel management or tourist service personnel, who may never read a book, but who must be able to communicate orally and readily with the people on whom their employment depends. If the teacher of a language class is able to sense the needs of his students, or if specific objectives are imposed by his school administration, he may need to revise and adapt the textbook he is using to fit needs other than those the author had in mind. He may want to discard material that doesn't lend itself to his objectives, or create supplementary materials for goals the author hasn't provided for. This kind of adaptation obviously has to begin with an analysis of the curriculum and of the proposed course text so that the two might be compatible.

A frequent requirement is the need to provide for oral-aural training, when vocal communication is felt to be important. We have discussed the concept of medium, with comparisons of the language forms that characterize differences in otherwise equivalent messages designed for oral and written communication. And these differences are important; failure to achieve congruence between medium and content is conspicuous, detracting from the efficient flow of ideas.

Suppose a curriculum objective specifies both oral and written competence, but the text provides only writing activity. A reading selection could be transposed into dialog form for use in the same lesson as the reading or in successive lessons. A significant difference between the two media is the give and take of conversation, where communication flows back and forth, compared with the essentially unidirectional stream presented in written form.

Note the following passage:

With rare exceptions studies of Spanish in the Southwest have suffered a lack of prestige. The local dialects were never really taken seriously and were considered of interest only as picturesque deviations from standard Spanish, or at best from standard Mexican Spanish. A special term of denigration has been developed to refer to these deviations and to those who use them: *pocho.* And it continues to detract from what could and should become an adequate regional standard.

The same content of this written selection can be presented in oral form. (Indeed, the "translation" from a written to an oral medium or vice versa may be an effective way to teach both.)

Roscoe: Why do you Spanish speakers from the Southwest often feel uncomfortable when you use Spanish with Mexicans?

Alfredo: Well, our local dialects are influenced by having been isolated, and by contact with English.

Roscoe: How so? In what way?

Alfredo: Mexicans laugh at us when we say *truje* or *vide*, because these are old-fashioned words that no educated Mexican would use.

Roscoe: I see, sort of like saying *anon* and *methinks* in English.

Alfredo: Yes, and even more annoying to the Mexicans is our use of loan words and phrases from English.

Roscoe: For example?

Alfredo: Well, like *baquiar* for *back up* (a car) and *casa de cortes* for *court house.*

Roscoe: Yes, I see the influence of English.

Alfredo: Sometimes, they're really bad, like *groserías* for *groceries.*

Roscoe: Why, what does *groserías* mean in Spanish?

Alfredo: *Vulgar insults!* No wonder the Mexicans call us *pochos.*

Another adjustment that calls for adaptation is the transition from what we might call intensive to extensive language teaching. Does the class cover a limited amount of material very thoroughly, or is a broader acquaintance with a wider range of material desired? The need is to achieve an appropriate balance between scope and time. In practical terms, the situation may call for the telescoping of a comprehensive language text so that it can be covered in a relatively brief period of time. Implicit in this process is the need to establish priorities on what is to be taught; that is, if time is limited, what should one give up? Approaching the matter from another point of view, we might need to determine how much a one-hour, five-day-a-week class can assimilate in four months, six months, one year, or two years. And in this connection, is it valid to assume that a one-year secondary school course is equivalent to a one-semester university course? Can university students really learn twice as fast? Obviously teaching philosophy enters into the adaptation equation.

If materials or a course must be condensed, goals must be restricted. One alternative is to proceed only part way through the textbook or syllabus. But there is often a strong desire to "finish the book," and rushing through the text, or the last part of it, may satisfy one's gestalt sense for the need of completion at the expense of mastery of the materials presented. Generally it would be preferable to cover a part of a text adequately (most are arbitrary in length and coverage anyway) than to provide only a fleeting glimpse of a longer course.

If some aspect of a fuller pattern of training must be sacrificed to the limitations of the time schedule, what should go? To answer the question one really needs to know the probable applications of language skills the students will make. If they exclusively (or near exclusively) need writing skills—or oral skills—the adjustments are self-evident. But more typically this cannot be fully anticipated. Secondary school classes, especially, contain many students whose future needs have not yet been articulated. As a result, a limitation of medium is often not possible. When a course outline or text that is too ambitious for the time available includes coverage of varying levels of usage, the best probable approach is a limitation of register and style. This can be illustrated from Joos' five levels (1962; also see Chapter 6 of this volume), listed and defined as:

5   oratorical—professional speakers
4   deliberative—large-group communication
3   consultative—formal, careful dialog
2   casual—informal, normal usage
1   intimate—communication with kin or close friends

If only one level can be attempted, it should probably be level 3, though level 2 is a close runner-up and is preferable in many situations. Third preference is level 4, not particularly useful.

Level 1 is of hardly any utility to second-language learners, except in the case of intermarriage; and the need for level 5 is even more rare. (In passing, it might be pointed out that the preference in some traditionally-oriented second-language classes is 4, 5, 3—with 2 and 1 purposely excluded from pedagogical orthodoxy, with a resulting limitation in utility, success, and motivation among learners.) Teachers should if possible aim for at least passive control of levels 2 and 4, even if active competence is limited to level 3.

There are other steps that can be taken to compress a textbook (or a course) into a limited time. One is very simple: move ahead any time the students are doing an activity well. Often there is a tendency to move slowly and enjoy the classroom successes. If a point has evidently been learned, skip ahead; it is not necessary to finish every drill, every section, every grammar point. Not only can exercises be left unfinished if students have satisfactorily mastered the patterns, some judicious skipping of entire points (those of limited usefulness) can be considered.

Expansion is much easier to arrange. It is relatively simple to add drills that elaborate on a point or pattern, introduce new vocabulary, enlarge the cultural relevance, etc. Several years ago we were involved with intensive language training in the Foreign Service Institute. Classes of various length per day were included in our schedule. The extremes were six hours a day and one hour fifteen minutes a day. It was our observation that there was nothing approaching five times as much accomplished in the longer class. In fact there was very little, if any, greater coverage of the material. There was actually considerable overlap: many students in the 75-minute class outperformed a substantial proportion in the 360-minute class, using the same teaching materials. We conclude that there is probably an optimum efficiency rate of perhaps two hours a day, beyond which additional gain is achieved at a substantially lower rate.

Another factor also deserves attention: students in the shorter classes came before the regular work day started, contributing half of the class hour from their own time, while students in the longer classes were on official assignment. Both groups were highly motivated, but the shorter class met in the fresh part of the morning, and most of these students had volunteered for training that, while work-related, was not required. They were definitely there because they wanted to be.

RECOGNIZING MOTIVATION AND APTITUDE

We are certainly not the first to observe that motivation is a crucial ingredient for successful language learning, and that incentives should be carefully considered. One curriculum practice which we suggest be avoided, if possible, is compulsory enrollment. We are convinced that to make a course obligatory often increases dissatisfaction and greatly reduces the chances of success. The same result of near-universal enrollment can often be achieved by affirmative incentives, which avoid the disinclination that naturally seems to spring up against imposed requirements. The carrot is definitely superior to the stick.

There are scholars who differentiate kinds of motivation, specifically distinguishing instrumental (desire to learn in hopes of a personal gain) from integrative (desire to become associated or identified with the culture the foreign language represents). There are two comments that seem relevant: (1) teachers rarely have any control over these factors, students in most language classes being clearly impelled by instrumental motivation, and (2) quantity and level are not specified—a high degree of instrumental motivation would certainly be preferable to a limited amount of integrative.

A lot remains to be learned about motivation, but a few simple general principles might be enunciated. First of all, a friendly interested teacher will motivate students far more effectively than a threatening, authoritarian individual. Empathy can produce superior results. Secondly, the self-fulfilling prophecy works both ways: expect a lot and students will produce (Rosenthal and Jacobsen 1968, pp. 19-23; Rist 1970, pp. 411-451). Thirdly, success breeds interest; offer an effective class and problems of motivation will be minimized. Finally, a teacher who is sensitive to individual differences and needs can adapt his approach and techniques to each of his students. The outgoing, aggressive student can be challenged, and the shy student quietly encouraged, thus successfully reaching and influencing the maximum number.

Along with motivation as a prime mover in language acquisition is aptitude, though some professionals suspect there is a strong positive correlation between aptitude and motivation. Indeed, perhaps they are two facets of the same phenomenon. Wanting to achieve a skill certainly enhances the likelihood of succeeding. Still, there appear to be individual differences in language-learning ability just as there are in more highly visible human traits. One fairly certain conclusion is that there are differences of learning styles and preferences, which can be related to differential results in the classroom. Some of these have their source in the neurophysiological make-up of individuals, depending on such factors as hemispheric dominance of the brain and handedness. The teacher normally has no control over these factors (short of a very sophisticated curriculum that measures such features and classifies students so they can be matched to preference). As a result, the best advice we can offer to the teacher is to provide a variety of activities and emphases, so there will be a greater likelihood that individual preferences and learning styles can be appealed to. Of course, variety in classroom activity can be good for its own sake. Certainly one important purpose of classroom adaptation is to provide a varied intellectual diet for students. (Davis 1967 suggests that the advantage of variety is a reason for preferring the early introduction of reading activities into an elementary school TESL program.)

ADAPTING NATIVE-SPEAKER TEXTS

We would like to present one final area of administrative and pedagogical concern: How should the traditional English teacher of native speakers of English respond if asked to take on the instruction of nonnatives? After all, he is a teacher of English, and competence in English is the goal sought, even though it is the student's second language. Certainly it makes more sense to approach English teachers than foreign language teachers. We still recall, though happily it is many years back, a Venezuelan being sent to a Spanish class in an American university because he didn't speak enough English to study architecture.

Not infrequently, the teacher of native English speakers almost panics when asked to teach English as a second language; he often asks for a book or a method to rescue him, thinking there must be an institutional solution to his problem. The remainder of this chapter is concerned with his plight. We attempt to outline specific differences in approach and requirements between first- and second-language instruction. A variety of concrete suggestions are made relative to the kind of modifications that are needed.

For one thing, the situation is different: accustomed to a student who knows the informal ranges of usage and needs to learn the formal ones (effective literacy and structural elaboration), the teacher is faced with a student who, if he knows any English, will very probably be completely innocent of any knowledge of the real language people use to communicate. Obviously the school should order appropriate English-as-a-second-language or bilingual textbooks. But in the meantime the teacher must start assisting her foreign students. If they are quite deficient, they will need to learn basic "classroom survival" English: *Go to Room 114, Come to the board,* and similar requests will have to be comprehended. They will need to learn how to ask a variety of questions in order to make their needs known and to respond orally to inquiries. When systematic study of the language is undertaken, they should have maximum opportunity for immediate application of what they have learned. Obviously the native speakers' text will have to be liberally supplemented and a number of areas postponed. The following discussion is aimed at outlining where the teacher will need to supplement or depart from the usual language instruction for natives in order to achieve congruence between materials and language learner.

Verb Phrases

When treating verbs, for instance, texts for native speakers provide instruction ranging from the use of vivid, concrete verbs for writing improvement to remedial work (eradicating *He done it, I could of gone*; engaging in annual forays against confusion with *lie/lay, sit/set, rise/raise*; and eliminating concord errors—One of the books *were* . . . , etc.)

The nonnative speaker has other needs and priorities. In *situational context,* he needs to learn the special properties of the verbs *be, have,* and *do.* He will learn that *be* is used to express time (*It's 8:30*), greetings, (*How are you?*), indications of profession and nationality, place (*It's over there*), color (*His house is green*), health, personal characteristics, age, dimensions, and mathematical expressions—since some languages use no verb in some of these situations or one verb in one situation and a second verb in another. He will note the use of *have* as a tense carrier, notably for the perfect tenses, when it is used as an auxiliary (and later its several forms as principal verb). He will become familiar with the functional applications of *do* in formulating questions and as a tense carrier (*He likes it* → *Does he like it?*), in negatives (*He likes it* → *He* doesn't like it), and later on its use in providing emphasis (*He* does *too live there*) and as a pro-verb used in questions to elicit an answer that is minimally a full verb phrase (*What is he* doing? / *Fixing his car*). Later, too, he must learn other important pro-verb functions (e.g., *She went shopping, and I* did *too*). Of course these points would not be taught as presented here. Even in early practice exercises, we would have something such as *Frank likes classical music, but Ann doesn't.* This observation applies to other grammatical illustrations given in this chapter.

The modal auxiliaries (*will/would, shall/should, can/could, may/might, must,* and *ought to*) will have to be acquired gradually since they present enormously complex problems to second-language students. While learning their many meanings, he will find them to be uninflected (except for present/past distinction as in *can/could*), and he will learn their special role as auxiliary verbs. Also to be gradually acquired are numerous two-word verbs (*He's* looking up *a friend*). Some of these, he will find, are separable (*I* looked *a friend* up *the other day*) but some not (not #*I* cared *him* for, *while he was ill*); personal pronouns *must* interrupt a separable two-word verb (*She* called *him* up but not *She* called up *him*).

In studying tense, the foreign student will find that *present* tense seldom expresses present moment (*Here he comes*), but rather general truth or situations (*I like steak*), customs, commands, future time (*He leaves tomorrow*), and occasionally historical present (*The audience applauds as Mark Twain walks to the platform*). In addition to some spelling complications in forming the third person singular (There is normally an *s* ending, but usually *es* is added to words ending in *o, s, sh, ch, x,* or *z*), pronunciation of the *s* inflection is slightly complicated: The student must learn that verbs ending in sibilants (*reach, fish,* and *dress,* for example) take the /-əz/ sound in the third person (*She dresses attractively*). But words ending in voiced consonants—other than sibilants—or vowels (*live, tag, go*) take the /-z/ when *s* is added; and *s* endings for words ending in voiceless consonants are pronounced /-s/.

While learning the various uses of the *past* tense, he will also gradually learn the many irregular verbs (*go/went, see/saw*). He will also be taught how to pronounce the *-ed* ending of regular verbs: /-əd/ for words ending in *d* or *t*   (*seat/seated*), /-t/ for voiceless endings other than *t* (miss/missed), and /-d/ for voiced endings other than *d* (*die/died, sag/sagged*). In addition, he will be made aware of compatible expressions with the past tense (such as *for, since, ago, before*).

Besides learning when to use the *future* tense, he will find that there are a number of ways to express the future: *will* (rarely *shall*) + stem, *be + going to* + stem (*is going to leave*), *be + about to* + stem, *be + to* + stem, present tense + adverb of time (*leaves tomorrow*), present progressive + adverb of time (*is leaving later*). Special verbs (such as *expect, hope, agree, decide, determine, plan*) combine with *to* + stem to express future ideas.

Use of the *perfect* tenses will prove to be more challenging than mastering the forms (*had sent, have sent, will have sent*). For example, students will learn not to use the present perfect when a definite time is mentioned (not *I have finished the book yesterday*); and as mentioned earlier, they will be able to choose between past tense and present perfect when they start to grasp the "aspect" meanings of verbs.

In learning verbs, the student will be taught to use appropriate contractions (*I'm, isn't, won't*) but not to use a contracted verb at the end of a sentence (not *Yes, he'll*). Besides passives, he will ultimately learn the difficult condition clause (*If he had known about it he might have . . .*). He will need to learn to move from direct quotations to reported speech (*George said, "I think I'll go"* → *George said he thought he'd go*).

He will study concord—agreement between subject and verb—and question forms with their special intonation, the question tag being particularly challenging. Here he will have to learn to produce a negative tag with a positive statement (*He* likes *math,* doesn't *he?*) and vice versa (*She* doesn't *live here any more,* does *she?*). In addition to concord in the tag, he will encounter the inconclusively irregular forms used for first person reference (*I'm doing very well, am I not/aren't I/right?*). Besides this, he will have to differentiate between and produce two different intonations: falling intonation when the speaker requests confirmation, and rising intonation when the speaker is seeking information.

Noun Phrases

Native speakers studying pronouns and nouns normally are drilled in case forms to eliminate errors such as *He talked with Jim and I.* Indefinite pronouns and compound noun subjects with *either/or,* etc., are studied to help the student with subject-verb concord (*Each of them is . . . / Either Frank or Carl is . . .*). Proper/common noun distinctions are made to aid in proper capitalization. Other categories, such as concrete and abstract, are studied simply because, like Mt. Everest, "they are there."

Often on the first day of instruction the *nonnative* speaker begins to work on pronouns (traditional training exposing him to *What's this?* questions and *It's a . . .* answers). In his exposure to personal pronouns, he learns of the two-case forms (*he* and *him*), then finds the genitive in the possessive pronoun category. He discovers anomalies such as *her* being used as objective form (*to her*) *and* possessive (*her book*), *you* covering both singular and plural situations, and *we* meaning the speaker and the listener, or the speaker and one other person, or the speaker and several others.

He sees that *-self* pronouns function one way as reflexives (*He cut himself*) and another way as intensives (*I'll do it myself*), with another form (*They laughed at each other*) being used in reciprocal situations. Relatives may be inflected (*who/whom*) or uninflected (*which, that*)—*that* operating in reference to people *and* things, but *who* and *which* with more specialized reference. Then he sees most of these pronouns in another role as interrogatives, *which* for example used as substantive or adjective (which is lost? *or* Which book is lost?) but *who* requiring a genitive (*whose*) to function as modifier. The demonstrative, he finds, has singular and plural forms (*this/these, that/those*) but no case. The indefinites are seen to have many forms (the *-body, -one, -thing* words plus *none, either, neither,* etc.); some of these, such as *everybody*, sound plural but require singular concord. The pronoun substitutes (distributives, quantifiers, enumerators) include *one* which can take modifiers (*the big, black ones*), ordinal numbers (*the first to arrive*), and other words expressing number or quantity.

By contrast, nouns seem less of a problem, except for their quantity. The concrete/abstract classification needs little if any attention; the common/proper distinction plays a minor role in connection with capitalization but a more significant one in the use of articles (*the boy*, but not *the New York*). The collective noun category (*The crowd was unruly*) has relevance in terms of subject-verb concord. The feature of compound nouns (*bookshop, postcard*) is useful in vocabulary building. "Case" is fortunately benign, there being only common and genitive. Irregular plurals constitute a challenge;

less of a problem is the pronunciation of the regular plural ending (/-s/, /-z/, /-əz/). Gender (*lion/lioness, niece/nephew*) creates little difficulty, but the differentiation between count nouns and noncount (or mass) nouns is a major hurdle:

a few tables *but* a little furniture
a few envelopes *but* a little paper
a few cookies *but* a little bread

Segments of noncount nouns can be enumerated with the appropriate "container" word:

tubes of toothpaste   *pieces* of furniture
bunches of grapes   *glasses* of milk

Spelling, concord, and capitalization also present some difficulty; but these matters cannot compare with the constant struggle to select the appropriate determiner. Earlier, the great complexity of the definite and indefinite articles has been touched on. *Few / a few, little / a little, some / any* are perennial problems. The nonnative speaker learns, for example, to associate *some* with positive statements (*He wants* some *dessert*) and *any* with negative statements (*We don't have* any *cake left*) or questions (*Is there* any *ice cream?*).

Modifiers

While native students are learning to select more "vivid" adjectives and to avoid the "degradation" of *more better* and *worser,* the nonnative speaker is again concerned with fundamentals. The *-er, -est* comparisons—even with the *more/most* complication with polysyllabics (*more beautiful*) is considerably less of a challenge than getting these modifiers in the right

order. *Both of the last two slender, gray-haired old men . . .*
comes with ease to the native but requires very extensive work
for the nonnative. Adverbial forms also pose considerable
difficulty. Working with experienced, well-trained but *non-*
native teachers of English abroad, we often hear, *Just, I would
like to ask you a question* instead of *I would just like to ask
you a question.* Structures involving comparison and contrast
require considerable exposure and assistance: *(bigger) than, as
(old) as, too (tall) for, too (cold) to, . . . is intelligent and Ruth*

is too (note also: *reads rapidly / is a rapid reader*; and *dog with*
curly *hair /* curly-*haired dog*). The student discovers that some
adjectives can function like nouns (the poor and the needy),
that nouns can often function as modifiers (a mud fence), and
that certain verb forms can function as adjectives (a very
promising report). He finds, too, the affixes which can
transform nouns to adjectives (*child/childlike, girl/girlish*) but
is warned about the frequent changes of meaning (*home/
homely* versus *home/homey*).

Connectives and Relaters

Young native speakers are trained not to use too many *and*'s
and *so*'s; others learn that a semicolon is needed before
conjunctions such as *therefore* and *nevertheless.* The nonnative
speaker requires extensive work simply to master the more
common prepositions and conjunctions:

    at home   *on* Center Street   *in* Louisville

and more effort to handle the less concrete

| *on* time | *at* odds with | *with* envy |
| *by* now | *in* trouble | |

We have noted how preposition-like particles occur as part of phrasal verbs (*call up, put on*). In addition, the nonnative speaker learns not only the various types of conjunctions (coordinating, subordinating, etc.) but also the semantic difference of *and* and *but,* the tense sequence in subordinate sentences (*After he*'d gone, *the rest of us finished* . . . or *After he went* . . .), and the various means by which embedding can take place (*He said something + He will come → He said that he'd come*).

In brief, while the language matters studied by the native and the nonnative speaker occasionally overlap, by and large they are of necessity concerned with quite different things. Often, areas such as mass and count nouns or use of articles are second nature to the native and therefore of no concern in an academic sense; yet these same matters are of paramount concern to the second-language learner. The teacher who suddenly finds it necessary to teach the nonnative should offer practical instruction which takes into consideration the special problems which we have just discussed. Such instruction will not stop with linguistic matters but will incorporate significant treatment of appropriateness, cultural awareness, and communicative competence. In short, the student's increasing linguistic competence will be recognized as an important ingredient—but only one ingredient—in the communication process.

APPENDIX INTRODUCTION

The appendices which follow are somewhat unusual. Rather than providing supplementary or explanatory details to our text, they present complementary studies by informed scholars on textbook analysis and evaluation for particular teaching-learning situations. More specifically, they can help the teacher answer the important question, "Can I teach successfully with this text?" (ideally without extensive adaptation).

One quite reliable way to judge a book is to evaluate it after having used it in a course. But this is time-consuming, and even a provisional adoption may mean that the book must be used for at least four or five years to justify the investment of funds necessary to acquire multiple copies. From an administrative point of view, the time to evaluate a text is clearly before it is adopted.

To provide the means for textbook evaluation independent of a classroom trial, we have turned to colleagues for assistance. Professors Hilferty, Bruder, and Tucker have been kind enough to permit us to publish their studies. The first two were especially written to appear in this volume. The third was originally published several years ago (*English Teaching Forum*, September-October 1968), but has never been easily accessible to professionals in this country. We are naturally very grateful to our three collaborators and to *ETF* for granting us permission to reprint.

We are also pleased that Professor Edward Fry has permitted us to include his "Graph for Estimating Readability— Extended," a tried and reliable instrument that can be most helpful in assessing the appropriate difficulty level of a textbook or reader.

We anticipate that these studies will be helpful in predicting whether a candidate textbook is usable. If the decision is affirmative, Chapters 1 to 9 of this volume can provide appropriate guidance to the curriculum specialist and to the teachers who choose and use the language text. For teachers in training, the appendix can serve as a convenient reference for evaluating and discussing the merits of language texts with varied emphases at a variety of levels.

Appendix 1
ADAPTING MATERIALS IN CONTEXT
Ann Hilferty

Choosing materials for an educational program without giving careful thought to the situation in which they are going to be used may not be quite as inefficient as shooting at a target while blindfolded, but it *is* inefficient. Whether the teacher or administrator is planning a new program, or maintaining one set up by someone else, or renovating a program of her own design, materials should be selected, adapted, and evaluated in the context of all considerations important to the design of the whole program.

GUIDELINES FOR SELECTING AND ADAPTING MATERIALS

The following list is suggested for preliminary reference when selecting or designing materials, and as a checklist when the materials have been adapted and put into use:

1. *Definition of the students.* The teacher should ask who the students are and what their purposes in school are. What are their backgrounds? their hopes? their reasons for learning

Ann Hilferty, coordinator, English Language Center at Northeastern University in Boston, directs the intensive English program. Ms. Hilferty has previously taught ESL and methods for teaching ESL in a number of Boston area universities, the Cambridge (Mass.) Public Schools and in Abeoauta, Nigeria.

English? Do they want to be scientists? mechanics? teachers? Do they want to participate in business? sports? the arts? Do they want to continue their education beyond high school? How much English and what kinds of English do they know already, and how much further do they have to go?

2. *The general instructional objectives.* These should reflect a set of values—the teacher's translation of the students' aspirations and the students' place in the school and the broader community. The objectives should be broad and idealistic, and might be shared by other courses in different fields. Their time frame might extend beyond that of the one specific course or program.

3. *The specific performance objectives.* These should be described as skills, easily observable and measurable, which act as samples from the wide array of skills the students will be capable of performing as the general instructional objectives are met. In addition to helping plan courses, performance objectives are useful as guidelines for evaluation during and at the end of the course. The abilities which these objectives represent are crucial to the attaining of the general instructional objectives, but they are usually specific to a particular course, and should be achievable during the time frame of that course.

4. *The conditions of the learning situation.* The teacher or administrator should consider conditions such as:
- The time—How many hours/days/weeks will the class meet? How much time do the students have, in the long run, to meet their goals?
- The logistics—What is the physical setup of the classroom? What else do the students participate in at the school?

5. *A statement of beliefs about learning and teaching.* This statement should include reflections on ways in which people learn, as well as opinions about the kinds of content, activities, materials, and programs which help to promote the development of the judgment and skills necessary for students' reaching the course objectives. The statement should include a

critical appraisal of the teacher's own style in teaching, and plans for developing that style further. It should contain a plan for a set of classroom protocols for teacher and students to follow consistently, and should give some attention to problems which can impede learning and possible solutions to those problems.

6. *The classroom calendar.* This should include plans for registration, testing and placement, class levels, syllabus, curriculum, and periodic and final evaluations. It should also include the setting of specific classroom objectives by week and day.

7. *The budget.* Almost nothing goes without saying. The teacher must ask questions like, "Who has to pay? How much do the materials cost? Does using the materials require training or special equipment?"

8. *The selection and adaptation of materials.* Decisions should be made about materials, because they seem to be the best possible available means to reach the goals set for the students under the conditions in which they must learn.

Putting the Guidelines to Use

In focusing on these considerations while choosing materials, the teacher clarifies her own understanding of the teaching situation and her beliefs in the potentials of students, teacher, and institution. Unless she is led to disastrous conclusions about a particular institution or class, the teacher should gain a sense of commitment and self-confidence which lead to habits of consistency and regular critical examination in teaching. The objectives and statements of belief support consistency in teaching, and the use of objectives and statements as guidelines and checklist supports the habit of critical examination. Of course, the guidelines themselves should be critically examined regularly.

Exactly how does one go about using major program considerations as guidelines? This depends on the structure and history of the program as well as on the teacher's style of concentration and the time available. For example, a teacher entering a large, tightly structured department might have only to familiarize herself with the conventions already established there, and then adapt her teaching to meet them, while a teacher starting an ESL course where one never existed before will have to define the major considerations by herself and proceed from there.

THE LANGUAGE TRANSITION PROGRAM: AN EXAMPLE

A particularly lucid example of materials selection, adaptation, and use done in a creative manner may be found in the history of the Language Transition Program, a public school program in ESL, in Lowell, Massachusetts, 1970-72. This program was one of the last exclusively ESL programs in Massachusetts, barely preceding the state government's decision to mandate Transitional Bilingual Education. The program served approximately 225 students ranging in age from five years to adulthood, from six areas of the world: Puerto Rico, Portugal, Greece, Italy, the Middle East, and French-speaking Canada. Program staff included a head teacher, thirty teachers, thirty teacher aides, and several support staff.

In a successful participatory effort, materials were selected and adapted as the program design itself was being developed. Although all of the teachers were certified, and many had taught before, few of them had had formal training in teaching ESL. The head teacher chose not to impose a program of someone else's design on the teachers, but rather to combine program planning with the training of the new teachers in a two-week workshop before classes began. Extensive dialog during this workshop led to agreement on major goals and the endorsement and adoption of a specific set of materials and a particular teaching method.

Preliminary Planning

First the teachers were introduced to the problems that were likely to arise in the new program with an extremely varied student population. After discussing the expected students and the possible compositions of the classes, the teachers as a group were able to set objectives and plan the program as follows:

General instructional objectives
- to develop a command of the four language skills, hearing, speaking, reading, and writing English, in order to continue education in the public school system and take part in everyday affairs
- to adapt to and take on the responsibilities of the Lowell school programs and take part in community life
- to develop fruitful understanding and work with the new and the established citizens of Lowell

Specific performance objectives
- to master the verbal and writing skills necessary for successful study at the appropriate grade level
- to master in particular the areas of greatest difficulty in learning the English language: English word order, the English verb system, the English prepositions, a basic utilitarian vocabulary, an abstract vocabulary, and idioms
- to successfully use the English-medium textbook at the appropriate grade level and for the appropriate subject area

These objectives were to be further articulated by each teacher as appropriate for her particular students.

Conditions of the learning situation
- The students were approximately 225 people, varying greatly in age, nationality, and educational background.
- The program was housed in a number of schools. Students were bused from all parts of Lowell to the schools, where they were to study English for the entire day until their command of the language was strong enough for them to join regular school programs in their neighborhood schools.

- The teachers decided to set a range of from six months to two years, within which time students were to strive to attain mastery of Basic English in writing and speech.

Selection of Materials

Keeping in mind the groups of specific students they were likely to be teaching, the next step for teachers was to decide on the tools to be used. It had been agreed that students would benefit most in the program by learning enough English to enable them to do school work in English, that is, to understand lectures and texts in English. The teachers further concluded that although they could not control the English students heard in the streets and playgrounds, they could control the English seen on the printed page, and they determined to limit themselves to teaching the English of the printed page in order for students to reach their course goals in the shortest time possible.

For these reasons, materials based on idiomatic spoken English were ruled out, and teachers had to look for more formal materials which contained graded linguistic structures and vocabulary. From a number of programs suggested and demonstrated by consultants, teachers selected the I. A. Richards, Christine Gibson materials, *English Through Pictures* for use throughout all levels of the program. In addition to satisfying the linguistics requirements of the design of the program and providing abundant classroom materials, *English Through Pictures* contained clear directions and consistent teaching techniques.

First published in 1945 and used internationally since then, *English Through Pictures* includes a set of three textbooks plus supplementary audio-visual and reading and writing materials. The materials embody a carefully-worked-out philosophy of language learning and teaching. They provide a format for their own use as well as many pedagogical suggestions, and they are eminently adaptable for use for beginning students of almost any age above five years, from any culture, and at many educational levels. In addition, the fastidious sequence of linguistic materials in the text provides, in effect, a list of micro-performance-objectives and criterion-referenced tests for daily classroom planning and evaluation.

Beliefs about Learning and Teaching

In discussions about learning and teaching, the teachers decided to endorse the position (1) that students ean learn language effectively by gaining strong control of a limited but serviceable number of words and sentence patterns with which they can communicate in most natural situations; (2) that students will learn this limited language most easily when it is presented to them in easily understandable sentences and groups of sentences presented in their simple linguistic forms, and when they can then practice the words and sentences in those patterns in a variety of modes; (3) that as the students learn increasingly difficult words and patterns they will see the ones learned earlier recur in increasingly complex uses; (4) and that when the students have mastered this limited English, they will be in a strong position to confront full English in everyday practical and academic settings.

This position is quite compatible with that of Richards and Gibson, whose beliefs about learning and teaching are revealed in the descriptions and suggestions for teachers in *English Through Pictures.* This deceptively simple, linguistics-based program is designed around the 850 words of Basic English and the sentence patterns considered by C. K. Ogden to be the most important in the language. The words and sentence patterns are presented in systematically graded steps. Only full-sentence forms are taught at first; question forms are postponed until Book II, because they so often elicit one-word answers. (It is, of course, possible to frame questions so that full-sentence answers are required. "Choice" questions, for example, can be so framed: *Will you be at home this evening, or is this the night your club meets?*) The authors claim that this restricted language can be learned in from six to twenty-four months, according to the learning speeds of the students.

All content is sequenced from simple/basic to more difficult/abstract. New words are presented first in their literal senses in ways which are physically demonstrable, and later in more abstract senses.

Meaning is supplied in the early stages through the use of drawings on every page, and teachers are encouraged to produce more of their own drawings. The authors aim at universal comprehensibility—thus the demonstrable sentences and the simple, stick-figure drawings. There is great ingenuity in the supplementary materials—they are simple, but designed to be used for a number of purposes each.

The teacher's most important task in presenting the materials is considered to be controlling the language as students practice increasingly difficult patterns. The teacher is urged to keep within the vocabulary and syntax of the text, and to keep her teaching materials and techniques free from ambiguity. After the teacher presents the materials orally with demonstrations and graphic aids, the students practice orally, and later do reading and writing exercises for reinforcement and the learning of additional skills. Students act out the sentences they are making, and practice with support materials to make up new sentences.

Teachers are urged to take advantage of all possible avenues of approach to the student without departing from the books' content—to have the students act out the sentences they are saying, and to read and write about and draw the sentences.

In spite of the program's sanction against the use of colloquial English forms as teaching points at this stage of learning English, teachers may depart from the text when talking to students, and may allow students to use language they learn outside the classroom, with corrections as needed. It is expected that every exchange between teacher and student will be completely understood by the student, and that the student will have a continuing sense of discovery in learning. Conscious analysis on the part of the student is not considered necessary at this level of language learning.

The teacher is expected to adopt and use consistently a set of teaching gestures and verbal directions, and to follow regular procedures in the presentation of new materials. She is advised not to repeat the new forms many times herself, but to have the students practice all new materials many times and in many different modes.

The authors contend that this limited, carefully graded presentation of English patterns will help the students gain habits of acceptable pronunciation and spelling in addition to strong control over the basic words and patterns of English. Although there is little room for modification of the books' linguistic content and sequencing, the program challenges teachers to use ingenuity while presenting the strictly organized content without sacrificing interest, and in a manner appropriate to a specific group of learners.

Further Details

The next step in the Language Transition Program was for teachers to define more specific goals for their respective classes, and to plan calendars.

The classroom calendar. A general time line suggested for the *English Through Pictures* materials was: college level, six months; high school level, one year; junior high and elementary levels, two years. Before they could write more specific objectives, teachers had to test their classes to determine levels of English proficiency and learning skills already acquired.

Supplementary materials. Teachers decided to make available a variety of supplementary materials—in order to reinforce the students' oral command of English, as well as to help them attain the literacy skills necessary to master the texts they would later be using in standard school programs.

The commercial and teacher-created materials included: teaching kits, written tests, story books, games, exercise books, workbooks, sentence and word cards, number books, coloring books, large and small pictures, graded readers, exercises, film loops, TV shows, and films. All these materials followed the conventions of the *English Through Pictures* books.

In addition, a reading program, also developed by Richards and Gibson and following the same program, was added. The reading program included a number of reading samples, strictly graded and presented one at a time to avoid reader confusion and build confidence. The program was designed, as were the language materials, to promote understanding of meaning as well as perceptual discrimination.

The budget. The costs of *English Through Pictures* plus supplementary materials and occasional consultants' fees were well within the program budget.

Final preparations. The remainder of the workshop was devoted to a more thorough introduction of these materials and practice in their use. First, the principles behind the materials were discussed, the materials presented, and ways of adapting them demonstrated. Then teachers grouped according to anticipated class ages and levels, to plan according to the needs of their students. Teachers familiarized themselves with textual materials, resource people, films, tapes, and supplementary audio-visual materials, and finally, they practiced peer teaching and making supplementary materials themselves.

Implementation and Evaluation

After the workshop teachers were on their own for a year with their assigned students. In some cases classes were held in "primitive" situations—in hallways, study halls, libraries, basements, and auditoriums. The head teacher visited each class initially, and later offered help in classes in which it was most needed. As a second level of adaptation, the head teacher found that teachers of widely differing personalities had successfully adapted the materials to suit their styles.

Students were tested every school marking period, and careful records of test results were kept. For purposes of student evaluation and placement, stages in the *English Through Pictures* materials were correlated approximately with grade levels of school work. The grade level attained by each student was usually one grade lower than the level she would be ready for if she were a native speaker.

A *summer followup program* at the end of the academic year included review of *English Through Pictures* materials as well as the introduction to English textbooks students could expect to be using in the regular school program the following year. During the summer program regular grade teachers helped the ESL teachers ascertain whether students were ready to study in English.

All but a few of the students in the program were ready for studies in the regular school system after being in the ESL Program for one year. At the end of the first year, a group of outside evaluators recommended it as a state and national model. Arguing from the demonstrated success of its graduates, the evaluators commended the program in particular for its realistic and precisely formulated objectives; the choice of well-organized methods and materials which allowed individualization in teaching as well as in learning; the group approach to program planning; and the two-week teacher-training/planning sessions at the beginning of the program. The evaluators' recommendations that more precise criteria be established for future teachers' Student Progress Reports, and that students be provided with more classroom hours and more structured experience outside the classroom only confirmed the program's basic goals and design.

DESIGNING AND EVALUATING A PROGRAM

Although the Language Transition Program is a clear example of careful, comprehensive planning, its administrative design is but one of many possible. Its ESL-only curriculum would not be accepted by some educators, and the particular school of Teaching English as a Second Language which it followed, like all schools of thought, would doubtless find critics if an effort were made to look for them.

The pervasive lack of agreement in the TESL community at large on the values and appropriate uses of available materials supports a strong argument for careful preparation before selection of materials. Materials and program designs should be selected or created and adapted because they seem to the selectors to be the best available means for students to reach goals.

Whether statements of purpose and goals have already been written by committees or administrators, or the ESL teacher is a committee of one charged with the responsibility of interpreting an institution's broadest educational objectives into a detailed program for ESL students, it is useful for even the experienced teacher or administrator to give careful attention to each of the steps, and to examine or re-examine each course as though it were about to be taught for the first time.

Those teachers or administrators who do not have the benefits of a group with whom to collaborate in the selection or adaptation of materials—or for the planning of an entire ESL program—may compensate by maintaining contact with others who are good teachers, or who are thinking and talking and writing about good teaching. ESL teachers are for the most part accessible to colleagues and generous in sharing ideas. It may even be helpful and advisable to invite an impartial (although sympathetic) observer into the classroom or program to do an evaluation.

A Planning Checklist

Here is one checklist for a program in ESL—one which would also serve as a useful guide in examining an existing program:

1. Identify and understand the students.
2. Clarify general instructional objectives.
3. Clarify specific performance objectives.
4. Articulate statements of belief about learning and teaching.
5. Describe the learning situation and set a calendar:
    a. Estimate students' present knowledge of English.
    b. Measure the time available and consider the resources.
    c. Plan a curriculum with checkpoints along the way.
6. Remember the budget.

7. Choose the texts and other materials which seem most clearly to suit goals for the students.
8. Plan to adapt materials to suit the class's needs.
9. Develop a teaching style and a classroom style. That is, adopt or devise a system of classroom organization and management, and a system of consistent teaching behavior which will stand the test of new ideas, whether adopted or rejected, and the strains of increasing complexity all programs experience after getting under way.
10. Write even more specific goals for students as the curriculum is planned from class to class.
11. Check your goals regularly by observing students' performance and by talking with colleagues and/or consultants.
12. Make an occasion, later, to go back to check whether all parts of the system selected, and all of the teaching materials chosen and adapted did indeed fit in with the principles of learning and teaching.

Setting Performance Objectives

Finally, here are some guidelines for setting performance objectives:
1. Express the objective in terms of the learner and the outcome, not the teacher and the process.
2. Identify the desired behavior by name, and describe the important conditions under which the behavior should occur.
3. Try to be neither too broad nor too detailed. If a performance objective is phrased well, (1) another person reading it will likely understand it in the same way that the author understands it, and (2) the phrasing will easily suggest a test specific enough to be appropriate for that objective alone.
4. Remember that the behavior described in an objective is a sample behavior which may be viewed as a partial indication of the degree to which a broader goal is being attained.

5. Limit each objective to one sample behavior. From one objective, it should be an easy step to test for the objective.
6. Arrange the objectives from simple to complex.

and to do a "really professional job":

7. Supply a time limit in which the objective should be reached.
8. Describe the minimum essentials for attaining the goal, and the maximum development which might be expected.
9. Define the important characteristics of performance accuracy.
10. Define the amount of acceptable deviation.

WORKS CONSULTED

Bloom, Benjamin S., ed. 1961. *Taxonomy of Educational Objectives,* V.I. David. New York: McKay Co. Inc.

Gibson, Christine. 1945. *Teachers' Guide for Learning the English Language.* Cambridge: Houghton Mifflin Company.

Gronlund, Norman E. 1970. *Stating Behavioral Objectives for Classroom Instruction.* New York: The Macmillan Company.

Johnson, Francis C., and Christina Bratt Paulston. 1976. *Individualizing the Language Classroom.* Cambridge: Jacaranda Press, Inc.

Mackey, William Francis. 1965. *Language Teaching Analysis.* London: Longmans.

Mager, Robert F. 1962. *Preparing Instructional Objectives.* Belmont: Fearon Publishers.

Richards, I. A. 1929. *Practical Criticism.* New York: Harcourt, Brace and World, Inc.

Richards, I. A. and Christine Gibson. 1962. *English Through Pictures,* Books 1-3. New York: Washington Square Press, Inc.

———. 1974. *Techniques in Language Control.* Rowley: Newbury House Publishers, Inc.

Steiner, Florence. 1975. *Performing with Objectives.* Rowley: Newbury House Publishers, Inc.

Appendix 2

EVALUATION OF FOREIGN LANGUAGE TEXTBOOKS: A SIMPLIFIED PROCEDURE

Mary Newton Bruder

In the past fifteen years the number of texts available for teaching foreign languages has increased at such a rate that there is a major problem of selection even for standardized or on-going programs. In addition there has been a proliferation of specialized programs (English for Special Purposes, English for Science and Technology) and programs in the "less commonly taught" languages accompanied by a surge in the number of texts available for such programs.

Two common practices for text selection are (1) in-depth analysis and (2) adoption on face validity, e.g., the text is laid out attractively and there seems to be enough material to meet curricular requirements. There are objections to both. A great deal of time can be wasted in a detailed, page-by-page analysis; and a great deal of money can be wasted if a text, adopted after a cursory check, proves unsuitable.

Mary Newton Bruder, Department of General Linguistics, English Language Institute—University of Pittsburgh, has taught foreign languages and ESL for 15 years, and has written materials and texts for ESL and teacher training.

USING THE EVALUATION CHECKLIST

What is helpful is a checklist so that the evaluator can quickly compare the texts available and at least narrow the field if not definitely choose the text for the specific situation. Upon completion of the checklist he should have sufficient information about the text to make the decision as to usability in his specific situation.

The checklist proposed (see p. 211) consists of eight categories to be considered in terms of the teacher who will use the text and the students who are to learn from the text. The checklist is broad enough for use by teachers of foreign and second languages in the U.S. and abroad and has been found to result in reliable inter-rater judgments of given texts for specified situations.

It should be emphasized that the checklist is not designed to eliminate texts of questionable or unsound linguistic analysis. Such texts must be discarded ahead of time. An examination of the grammatical rules and explanations is one way to check the analysis. For example, I would not consider usable a text for teaching English which included as a teaching point the *shall/will* "rule." Nor would I want to use a text for a Romance language which taught only the familiar form of the second person. Texts for teaching speaking skills should be examined for native-speaker naturalness of language. *"La plume de ma tante est sur la table,"* adequately illustrates a teaching point, but hardly reflects the usage of a native speaker of French.

Once unsound texts have been eliminated, the evaluator can compare the rest in terms of a specific teaching-learning situation. No text can be effectively evaluated in a vacuum. One must know or be able to hypothesize fairly concretely the classroom situation, which includes the teacher's background and experience and the students' needs and interests.

Briefly, the technique is to consider the criteria from the point of view of the teacher and text as well as from the point of view of the student and text. Assign a plus (+) if there is a match, a minus (−) if there is a mismatch, and a zero (0) if the text can be adapted.[1]

EVALUATION CHECKLIST

Subject: *English as a foreign language*

Criteria Text	MESG	CEFC					
1. Level Comments	+	+					
2. Objectives Comments	+	+					
3. Style Comments	+	+					
4. Language background Comments	+	+					
5. Age Comments	+	+					
6. Time Comments	+	+					
7. Convictions Comments	−	0					
8. Competency Comments	+	−					

Evaluated for:
Teacher:____X, Y, Z_____
Native Language:___Gateauan___
Experience:___2 years_____

Class:___nonintensive_____
Native language:___Gateauan_____
Level:___beginning—intermediate__
Age:___high school_____
Location:___Lower Gateau_____

The chart is merely a device for organizing the data and simplifying the comparison of many texts. The space for comments is provided as a memory aid when comparing many texts. The usual practice at the English Language Institute is to have a number of people evaluate the texts independently and then meet as a group for discussion. Clearly two evaluation sheets for a given text will be divergent if the teaching situation is considerably different, but the score sheets from different evaluators for the same teaching situation virtually always agree in most significant aspects.

It is not intended that the pluses and minuses be added to arrive at the "best" text, although the temptation to do so is very strong. Each evaluator knows best his own situation and should give more weight to those criteria which are most important to him. In practice, however, any text which receives a minus for the "level" criterion can safely be dismissed from further consideration.

A Hypothetical Case

For the purpose of illustration, let us suppose that we are curriculum coordinators reviewing grammar texts for teaching English in Lower Gateau. The teachers are native speakers of Gateauan who were trained in Gateau and have been teaching for at least two years. The students are in high school and have studied English as a foreign language for one year. They are at the beginning—intermediate level. Because it is a developing nation, the Gateauan government has an extensive program for training its students at technical schools in the United States once they have completed high school in Gateau. (This information has been filled in on the chart, see page 211.)

We have received copies of eight texts for consideration, two of which will be used here as examples. The first, entitled *Modern English for Students in Gateau (MESG)*[2] is, according to its preface, based on "scientific principles of linguistic descriptions of English and Gateauan" and employs "the most modern principles of language teaching theory." The second, entitled *Contemporary English for Communication (CEFC)* is based on "scientific principles of linguistic description" and the "most modern principles of language learning theory."

Upon further investigation *MESG* turns out to be a fairly traditional audio-lingual text based on a contrastive analysis of English and Gateauan, while *CEFC* seems to be based at least in part on transformational grammar (there are ➔ 's and terms such as "Cleft sentence," and rules are described as "processes"). The preface of *MESG* states that the text is designed for use by intermediate students of English and that of *CEFC* promises a text for students at the beginning and intermediate levels.

Now let us consider these texts for our specified class in terms of the eight criteria. The first six will concern the students and the texts, the last two, the teacher and the texts.

1. *Level.* The level of the text in terms of grammatical structures, lexical items, reading passages, etc., should match the proficiency and interests of the students. Checking the preface, the sequenced list of the grammatical structures in the table of contents, and the length of the productive utterances is the easiest way to determine whether or not the text is too difficult for the students. For example, a (+) is assigned for a beginning text and beginning students; a (−) for a beginning text and advanced students. A (0) can be assigned for a text which overlaps the students' proficiency, i.e., it begins lower and ends higher than the proficiency of the students. In each of our hypothetical texts, the level is appropriate and each receives (+).

As mentioned earlier, a (−) in this category is sufficient to exclude a text from further consideration.

2. *Objectives.* Consideration of the students' objectives for taking a language course is second only to the level of a text. A text designed to teach conversational skills to a student who needs to pass a written standardized exam as a graduation requirement is probably not going to be very successful, and it would receive a (−) on the scale. On the other hand, a text which emphasizes reading and writing would receive a (+) for the same student. A (0) should be assigned in a situation where the student needs a particular skill but uses a text which presents all the skills. In this situation, some of the material is useful to the student, and there is the possibility for

supplementation. Both hypothetical texts offer all skills which our Gateauan students need and thus receive (+) marks.

3. *Language style.* Style, as I use it here, includes both register and dialect. The student who will study at a university in the country of the target language may need to learn a different language style from the one who remains at home and deals with visiting tourists.

Since our students from Gateau will study at universities in the U.S., the conversational style should include both the formal and informal registers as well as American English dialect. A (0) might be assigned to a text with formal British, for while it is not exactly what the students will need, they would certainly not be seriously handicapped. Both texts under consideration here rate a (+) in this category.

Note however, that the attitudes of the native speakers toward dialects of their language is an important consideration in some cases. Many Americans consider British English as "superior," so that a student in the U.S. with a "British accent" may be admired, whereas a student in England with an "American accent" may not be so favorably regarded.

4. *Language background.* Some texts are based on a contrastive analysis of the target and native languages, while others are based on a linguistic analysis of only the target language. One important thing to consider when evaluating C.A.-based texts is the language (native or target) in which directions and explanations are given. Using a linguistically sound text based on a C.A. other than the students' native language is not harmful as long as the explanations are in the target language.[3]

In our hypothetical case, *MESG* would receive a (+) since it uses English and Gateauan C.A. as a basis. Texts would be marked (0) if the contrast basis and the students' native language are near, e.g., a text in English for Spanish speakers used with students whose native language is Portuguese. As mentioned above, texts with a C.A. not near the native language, but totally written in the target language, will also receive a (0) for this category. A text receives (−) if it is based on a language totally unrelated to the students' and contains rules and explanations in the unrelated language—e.g., a text for Spanish speakers, containing rules and explanations in Spanish, for use with students whose native language is Japanese.

Texts based solely on the target language can only receive a (+) in this category because, theoretically, the text should be usable in any situation for which it is on the correct level. This is the case with our fictitious *CEFC*.

5. *Age*. Contextual situations and lexical items hold differing interest for the students depending upon their age; the material in the texts must be appropriate to the learners' age.[4]

A text receives (+) if it is appropriate for the students in all respects, e.g., university situations and lexicon for students who are academically oriented; (−) if it is totally inappropriate, e.g., an academic text in an elementary classroom; and a (0) if only partially appropriate but adaptable by the teacher.[5] In our fictitious case, the vocabulary and situations are appropriate to young adults, so each text receives a (+) in this category.

6. *Time*. The time element must be considered because materials designed for intensive courses (a minimum of 15-20 classroom hours per week) are sometimes quite different from materials for a "three hours a week" course. Intensive course materials do not require so much specific review because the students do not have so much time between sessions to forget and, therefore, a great deal more material can be presented in a given number of hours. If the text can be used to teach what the student must know in the time allotted, then it receives a (+); if not, a (−); if it can be adapted, a (0). Since both *MESG* and *CEFC* are designed for a nonintensive program and contain plenty of review material, each receives a (+).

7. *Convictions*. This criterion refers to the linguistic and pedagogical principles on which the text is based and the linguistic training and pedagogical approach of the teacher.

If our teachers in Gateau have been trained in structural linguistics and are adherents of the behavioral approach to learning, then *MESG* will receive a (+), and *CEFC*, a (−). On the other hand, if they are followers of the cognitive-code theory and of T-G linguistics, then the marks will be reversed.

A third situation, where both texts receive (0), is that of teachers who have been trained eclectically to select the best of all theories and to supplement any given text for use in the classroom. Selection of a text with a (0) in this category should take into consideration availability of supplemental materials or of skilled teachers who have time and training to create the necessary materials.

The Gateauan teachers have studied languages themselves by means of the grammar-translation approach and are firmly convinced of the value of learning grammatical rules. On this basis, *MESG*, the audio-lingual text without rules or explanations, receives a (−); whereas *CEFC*, which looks similar to the traditional texts but which is not based on a familiar learning theory, receives a (0).

A note of caution should be added here about individual teacher preferences. If the teachers do not like a text for some reason, it is almost certainly doomed to failure. There are many reasons why teachers take a dislike to certain texts: the grammar explanations may be confusing; or there may be cultural stereotypes which offend certain teachers. Whatever the case, if the teacher does not like the text, the attitude will be quickly picked up by the students. Whenever feasible, classroom teachers should be actively included in the evaluation and selection processes.

8. *Competency.* Teacher competency in using a particular text depends on his proficiency in the target language, his training, and his experience. Upon careful examination, we find that the prospective user of *CEFC* must have a high proficiency in English and should be familiar with the terminology of T-G linguistics. Thus, for a teacher who has no training in linguistics and has only an average proficiency in English, *CEFC* must receive a (−), whereas *MESG* might well receive a (+), which turns out to be the case in Gateau.

A (0) should be assigned in this category only when the characteristics of the teacher are doubtful or unknown, but where the program has a supervisor trained in linguistics who is capable of helping teachers with texts which they find difficult.

Summary remarks. The evaluators in our hypothetical situation now face a difficult decision. Clearly neither text is perfect for the student. *MESG* is usable by the teachers in terms of the language proficiency required, but they may resist using it. *CEFC* would be better received, but would probably require too much preparation for the individual teachers.

One solution would be to continue to look for a text which better matched the situation. Another would be to adopt *CEFC* for a class or two and assign the most proficient teachers to teach from it. A third would be to adopt *MESG* and provide supplemental explanations and rules. The choice of solution depends on availability of funds and trained and experienced personnel, neither of which are in plentiful supply in Gateau. The evaluators would probably choose the first solution and continue the search.

Our experience in using the checklist usually results in a much more cut-and-dried decision; most texts are eliminated on student-text factors such as "level" and "objectives." I have chosen a particularly complicated (but far from unusual) situation in order to illustrate all of the factors involved in text evaluation and adoption.

NOTES

1. Zero (0) should not really be considered a "bad" mark—more a neutral one.

2. At the time of writing these titles are purely fictitious.

3. The Lado-Fries Series (University of Michigan Press), based on a Spanish-English contrastive analysis, was used in English classes around the world.

4. We once had a call from a layman who had volunteered to help a 45-year-old East European learn English. The caller could not understand why her child's elementary school reader should have failed so miserably with the man.

5. One recently very popular series features university students in a proper setting, but the vocabulary is appropriate to ten-year-olds.

Appendix 3

EVALUATING BEGINNING TEXTBOOKS

C. Allen Tucker

As classroom teachers, supervisors, or members of a textbook committee, many of us have had the responsibility of evaluating beginning textbooks for English as a second language. I suspect that often we have undertaken such an evaluation reluctantly and with the feeling that we weren't sure what to base our judgments on, how to qualify these judgments, or how to report the results of our assessment. In short, we found ourselves lacking an efficient, systematic approach to evaluation.

A system for evaluating beginning texts should, I believe, include the following components:

First, the system should include a comprehensive set of criteria consistent with the basic linguistic, psychological, and pedagogical principles underlying currently accepted methods of language teaching. They should be exhaustive enough to insure assessment of all characteristics of the textbook. And they should be discrete and precise enough to focus attention on one characteristic at a time or on a single group of related characteristics.

Dr. Tucker currently serves as Associate Professor of Applied Linguistics and Director of the Language Institute at Florida Institute of Technology. He has also served as a consultant to San Francisco Public Schools, Encyclopedia Britannica, University of Florida and numerous other organizations and institutions. Dr. Tucker earned his PhD from the University of California at Los Angeles.

Second, the system should include a flexible rating scheme that provides a method for the comparative weighting of the criteria and a simple system for recording the evaluator's judgments on each—a system that reflects both the comparative weight of the criterion and the book's assessed merit as measured by that criterion. Further, the rating scheme should be flexible enough to be adapted to the special requirements of any teaching situation.

Third, the system should provide a rating chart that facilitates a quick, easy display of the evaluator's judgment on each criterion and presents a graphic profile of the total evaluation. Finally, it should provide a visual comparison between the evaluator's opinion of the book and a hypothetical ideal.

EVALUATIVE CRITERIA

A body of criteria for textbook evaluation can be organized in numerous ways. For the system suggested here, the criteria have been divided into four categories: Pronunciation, Grammar, Content, and General. The criteria are numbered consecutively to correspond with their number on the chart, given later in the article.

Pronunciation criteria

Evaluation of the presentation of pronunciation requires attention to three important criteria:

1. *Completeness of presentation.* A complete presentation of the pronunciation of English requires two essential ingredients: the sounds, and the suprasegmental signals (stress, pitch, intonation, juncture).

Presentation of the sound system must include the full range of vowels and diphthongs. Present in practically every syllable, they are probably best presented first. Where the age of the learner permits, information about the point and manner of articulation should accompany the subsequent presentation of the consonants. Hopefully, some systematic grouping will be evident in presentation of the consonants. Groupings such as stops, fricatives, and nasal resonants, with the voiced/voiceless distinction made wherever it applies, is better than a presentation in terms of alphabetical position. Again, where the age of the learner makes it practical, the presentation of a suitable system of phonetic or phonemic symbols may facilitate both text and chalkboard display.

Since the suprasegmental signals are so extensive in English and contribute so much to meaning as well as to correct rhythm and pronunciation, they should be presented as fully as the age of the learners permits. This presentation should include information, examples, and practice on basic sentence intonation patterns, word and sentence stress, coincidence of pitch and stress, and juncture.

A complete presentation of English pronunciation will include considerable attention as well to the practice of reducing unstressed vowels and the consequent substitution of schwa /ə/ or barred-*i* /ɨ/ in unstressed positions. Since the rhythm of spoken English depends so much upon a correct application of this concept, its presentation is an important item.

Some texts leave far too many of the problems of English pronunciation to the teacher. Often the teacher is not capable of supplying this information adequately. If the book is designed for learners too young to benefit from the more complicated aspects of the pronunciation system, they should be included in a teacher's text, guide, or handbook.

2. *Appropriateness of presentation.* The book must be evaluated in terms of the appropriateness of the presentation of pronunciation for the situation in which it is to be used. Beginning texts will divide into at least four categories in terms of their presentation of the sound system.

First, they will divide into two groups based on the background of the student. If the book is for students from a single language background, it should present a contrastive analysis of the sound system of English and that of the native language. It should emphasize drill sequences of minimal-pair words and utterances that illustrate the sounds and combinations most difficult for the student because of interference from his native language. But if the book is for students from a heterogeneous background, its presentation of the sound system must be based on an analysis of English, with special emphasis on those sounds that have been found to be especially difficult for most learners of English.

Second, beginning texts can present the sound system in one of two ways, depending on the age of the student. The book for younger students can leave more to the teacher and to the technique of imitation in presenting linguistic and phonetic details and terminology. If diagrams or drawings of the voice mechanism are included, they should be appropriate to the age and level of the learner and clearly and simply labeled. On the other hand, if the text is for learners who are literate in a common background language, much of the information about pronunciation can be given to them in their native language, especially in the earlier parts of the text.

3. *Adequacy of practice.* Materials for pronunciation practice must be adequate in both quality and quantity. Vocabulary lists to be pronounced after the teacher do not insure adequate pronunciation practice because such lists may not take into account the learner's difficulties with pronunciation, nor do they provide suitable context for word practice. Beginning with the initial presentation of the sounds and continuing throughout the text, all pronunciation practice should be presented in a context. That is, individual sounds should be practiced in words and words should be practiced in sentences.

Sounds that are difficult for most learners or for learners from a specific language background should be initially presented for practice in series of minimally different words. Subsequently, such practice may be in sentences, conversations, or dialogs. Similarly, problems of word stress and vowel reduction, along with sentence rhythm and intonation, require a great number of illustrating and contrasting sentences for practice. The pronunciation materials presented in, or accompanying, the text should include a sufficient number of drill words and sentences related to the vocabulary and structures presented in the lessons.

In summary, it is particularly important that the various aspects of pronunciation be *practiced*—not merely talked about—and further, that pronunciation drill materials be provided in the back rather than left to the teacher.

Grammar Criteria

In applying grammar criteria, the evaluator is concerned with how much of the structure of the language is presented, how well it is presented, and how readily the student may be able to benefit from the presentation.

4. *Adequacy of pattern inventory.* The variety, extent, and quality of language patterns presented should be carefully considered. The text should include the basic patterns necessary for using the language up to whatever level of complexity the book achieves, and the structural features introduced should contribute to that goal. While a quick look at the table of contents may suggest the extent of the pattern inventory, a careful examination of the lessons might reveal that the presentation and practice of patterns is clumsy, obscure, fragmented, or faulty.

If the level of sentence complexity presented in the text does not go beyond simple sentences, there is obviously little need for a full presentation of the conjunction system. But, in any beginning text, a fairly full range of prepositions, along with adverbs, adjectives, and possessives, is necessary. The function of nouns as modifiers distinguished from compound nouns, as in *gold ring* versus *gold mine,* and a clear distinction between mass and count nouns are examples of additional desirable patterns.

In summary, the pattern inventory is adequate to the extent that it presents the patterns possible within the limits of the book's terminal level. And the patterns presented are of adequate quality if they reveal the forms and characteristics of the various sytems of which they are members.

5. *Appropriate sequencing.* Since organization is so necessary to language learning, a primary function of instruction is
to present the language in a way that helps the student either
to understand the textbook's organization or to develop his
own. In the case of a beginning textbook, these purposes are
best served by a careful sequencing of the levels of structure so
that the introduction of new structures or patterns rests upon
a foundation of simpler patterns and structures already
mastered.

Except where functional load would indicate otherwise,
presentation of sentence patterns, modifier structures, and
vocabulary should move gradually from the simple to the more
difficult. Simple sentence patterns like Subject—Intransitive
Verb—Adverb, and Subject—Verb—Noun are suitable for early
lessons and should be thoroughly learned before more complicated patterns are introduced and before modifying structures
are attached to them.

In a similar way, question transformations should be
presented in a graded sequence. Probably the simplest form of
question is the inversion of *That is a clock* to form *Is that a
clock?* Other types of questions, involving more complex
transformations, should be presented subsequently according
to the order of difficulty.

Regular verbs are best dealt with first, except where
functional load requires the use of high-frequency irregular
verbs. *To be,* of course, must be presented very early in the
course despite its irregularity. The present continuous is
probably the most functional tense for early use.

Among the pronouns, subject pronouns are needed first.
Depending on the sequencing of related structures, the other
pronouns may be taught in almost any order.

6. *Adequacy of drill model and pattern displays.* An
evaluation of the book in terms of this criterion involves
making a judgment about how readily the student can discern
the form and content of a new pattern and can discover what
is expected of him in the various drills and pattern practices. If
the book is to be easy for him to follow in this respect, it must
present simple, self-explanatory initial displays of each new

pattern. Also, it must show him the kind of pattern substitution, alteration, or response required of him in a drill.

These displays are best understood by the student of a beginning text if they make use of boxes, arrows, contrasting colors and type faces, and other graphic devices rather than lengthy explanations. Also, the age or level of the learner must determine the appropriate level of complexity of such displays. Labels and grammatical identifications should be kept to a practical minimum. Wherever necessary, they should be expressed in simple terms, and a term once used should be consistently adhered to.

7. *Adequacy of practice.* Genuinely adequate practice of patterns and structures requires drills and practice exercises which are meaningful, appropriate for their purpose, and sufficiently diverse. A book that parades a wide variety of drill types in each lesson may include among these drills many that require of the student only the tiresome repetition of a single word or phrase in a long list of sentence contexts. In such cases, quantity does not guarantee adequacy. The student should be practicing what he is expected to learn, and while it may be true that elementary language learning is more a matter of habit formation than of problem solving, mere repetition in a number of unlikely or ridiculous contexts is apt to prove unproductive.

Good drills frequently require the student to make a variety of responses and discriminations which are representative of the decisions and productions necessary in actual speech. Appropriate drills provide the variety necessary to permit student practice of the range of behavior that is relevant to the structure or structures being practiced. On the other hand, exercises which test knowledge of the language should not be mistaken for exercises which give practice in using the language; testing exercises are not practice exercises.

Content Criteria

Lessons in pronunciation and grammar require the use of the language as content. The actual vocabulary presented, the situations discussed, and the semantic contexts used to impart additional meaning within the lesson comprise an important element of the book.

8. *Functional load.* The problem of functional load is, actually, a problem created by the extent to which certain difficult and complex words and structures are essential to the manipulation of the language or to its minimal use in communication. Some irregular forms, complex structures, or patterns which are hard to explain, such as greeting formulas, must be presented early in the book. They should be presented as formulas to be learned without explanation. For example, the introduction of *to be* presents many problems to the learner because of its irregularity, even in the simple present. But, because one cannot say *I am the teacher* or *How are you?* without it, the functional load of *to be* justifies its presence very near the beginning of the course.

Similarly, the introduction of vocabulary must conform to the requirements of functional load. Complex expressions used in telling time, counting money, and naming the days and months are necessary very early, if dialogs and drills are to approximate real conversations. The same justification can be extended to the inclusion of such idiomatic expressions as *I feel fine* and *All right.*

The textbook which is prepared for an adult learner in specialized circumstances may exhibit special functional load requirements for technical vocabulary of a trade or profession.

In summary, the presentation of vocabulary and patterns of the language should follow a scheme of logical sequencing, derived from the basic structure of the language, unless the special requirement of functional load dictates otherwise.

9. *Rate and manner of entry and re-entry.* Application of this criterion should be extended to both vocabulary and grammatical structures. Suitable entry involves economy and timing. Both vocabulary and structures should probably be introduced sparingly in early lessons. Some texts introduce six words and one or two structures in the first lesson. The optimal number depends upon the age of the learner and the

length of the lesson in terms of class minutes or hours. The number may increase in later lessons. Some texts that introduce six new words in the beginning lessons will introduce twelve in the later lessons. The number of structures presented may increase somewhat, too. However, for most beginning learners, a one-hour lesson probably cannot effectively present more than three structures, depending upon their complexity.

The concept of economy also applies to re-entry. Once a word or structure has been introduced, it should continue to play an active role. Some vocabulary and some structures are capable of much more frequent use than others. However, even the less adaptable items should reappear from time to time. Although introduction formulas need not be a part of every lesson, they can occasionally reappear in different dialog and narrative contexts. A verb tense, once introduced, can play a very steady part in the majority of the lessons. In particular, a given tense may reappear as an aid to practicing a subsequent new verb tense.

Timing of entry and re-entry is deserving of some scrutiny. Suitable entry is, like sequencing, a matter of careful arrangement with special attention to the adjacent items. Confusingly similar vocabulary or structures should not be introduced in close proximity. For example, the introduction of *they are* and *there are* in the same lesson is very confusing to most students.

Common to most current methodology is the audio-lingual approach to the sequencing of language skills. According to this approach, all new material should be presented first in an oral practice, a dialog, or a narrative portion of a lesson, so that the student hears and repeats it before he looks at the printed words. A book organized in such a way that this kind of presentation is difficult or impossible does not lend itself to the audio-lingual approach to language teaching.

When items reappear, they should often do so in somewhat different contexts and situations in order to facilitate learning their range of applicability in English. The uses of verbs like *make* and *have*, and of prepositions, for example, can be gradually expanded by re-entry in slightly different contexts which exemplify new environments. Re-entry is closely related to sequencing. Re-entry in new contexts, therefore, usually presupposes re-entry in more complex structures and in larger patterns. The re-presentation of a word or simple structure always in the same kind of sentence or frame is inconsistent with the concept of a sequential increase of difficulty.

10. *Appropriateness of contexts and situations.* The content of the text can be evaluated in terms of both pedagogical and cultural appropriateness. The context of an oral practice, narrative, or dialog should be prepared in such a way that a variety of natural English utterances can be used to introduce the vocabulary and structures to be taught in that lesson. Certainly, a dialog format provides better opportunity for introduction of a new question pattern than a narrative oral practice would. Also, the content of narratives, dialogs, etc., can help to establish the meanings of the words and phrases that are introduced.

Content material should be suited to the age, level, background, and interests of the students. Young children are easily bored with "talky" narratives, while older students may intellectually reject childish dialog. In general, interesting material presented in vocabulary and structures that the student can control with a steady rate of increment will likely prove to be the most appropriate pedagogically.

The contents of oral practices and dialogs and the situations discussed therein can contribute meaningfully to the general presentation of the culture of English-speaking peoples. If the learners are likely to live in, or visit, an English-speaking country, an expanding cultural insight should be one goal of instruction. And since effective control of the language requires at least a minimum of knowledge of the cultural implications in formulas, idioms, etc., presentation of the culture is really inescapable.

However, if the text is designed for an area where English is taught as a second language for use as a medium of instruction, the learner is likely to need and want considerably less of the target culture. Rather, the content will be more appropriate for him if it is developed from a contrastive analysis of the two cultures and gives considerable weight to his native culture. Also, if the text is designed for learners from a single language background, its contents should be carefully controlled to avoid situations which offend local sensitivities or violate cultural taboos.

General Criteria

The remainder of the criteria require a broader view of the book and frequently involve assessing factors that are external to the volume itself.

11. *Authenticity of language.* The language used in a beginning text must, for simplicity's sake, be confined to a narrow range of style and functional variation. Since the language which is being taught is the spoken language, the tone of language used in the text should be that of standard spoken English. Idioms and idiomatic usage are necessary and advisable, but sub-standard dialects, slang, and obscure regional idioms should be avoided in a beginning text.

12. *Availability of supplementary materials.* If a language lab, tape recorder, or record player is available, supplementary pronunciation and pattern-drill tapes or discs might be very helpful. If available teachers are not adequate models of spoken English, such audio supplements become even more advisable. Also, pictorial display materials for picture practice may be available. Other things being equal, the text whose publisher offers these and similar supplementary aids may offer some advantages over competing volumes.

13. *Adequate guidance for non-native teachers.* Quite apart from supplementary materials is the problem of sufficient guidance for the non-native teacher. If the teachers are unlikely to have native competence in English or sufficient training in modern methodology, the text should be accompanied by a teacher's edition or guide with adequate simplified guidance for presenting the varied ingredients of the text. In

some cases, the guide or handbook may include some background on current methodology and suggestions for classroom activities and techniques. For some teachers, assistance in point and manner of articulation of English sounds and exposure to a phonetic alphabet may be helpful. Where a variety of texts are available and roughly comparable, tailoring the choice to the needs of the teachers in terms of teacher guidance may serve to increase the quality and decrease the burden of the teaching.

14. *Competence of the author.* The question of the author's competence is largely answered through an examination of his product, the textbook. However, knowledge of an author's reputation and previous works may be helpful in the following ways: (1) If the evaluator has rated the book highly on a significant number of important criteria, then the name of a recognized and respected author tends to confirm this favorable assessment. (2) If the evaluator believes the author to have previously produced some unsound works, this should point to a more rigorous scrutiny of the judgments made. If the author is unknown to the evaluator, a bit of investigation will reveal his standing in the field. In the final analysis, of course, the book should be accepted on its own merits. The name of a highly esteemed author is of little value on the jacket of a book that appears to be unsuitable.

15. *Appropriate level for integration.* If the text under consideration is not part of a series, all of which is being considered, then the question of how well it will fit with the text for the following course must be asked. An examination of the early lessons in the following course will give a good indication of what competency in English is assumed there as entering behavior for the students. This assumed competence then becomes the measure of a suitable level of instruction which this text should contribute to. For example, if in the beginning of the text for the next course, the present perfect tense is used in dialogs and is not taught, then that tense should have been taught in the preceding text. A similar comparison of the complexity of sentences, level of vocabulary, and emphasis on composition and reading will serve to

indicate how well the text being evaluated will contribute to the necessary entering behavior for the following course. A certain amount of overlap is desirable. The initial lessons in a second course may profitably represent material covered late in the previous course. However, if this overlap is too extensive, little learning and considerable boredom may result.

16. *Durability.* The more expensive hard-cover text is often considered to be the most durable type. A careful examination may reveal weak or wide-spaced stitching in the binding, lightweight or easily breakable hard board in the covers, or shoddy fabric used as cover material. The best of the hard covers reveal their durability through the absence of these shortcomings. Plastic-impregnated fabrics provide the most durable covers because they are stain and dirt resistant, as well as washable.

A good soft-cover (paperback) text may be much more durable than a poorly bound hard cover. Although the cover will inevitably show use faster than a hard cover, the soft-cover text may stand many a semester's use. The most durable soft-cover book has a sewn or stapled binding with a sturdy fabric backbinding. Such books do not lose their pages like the texts with a glued binding. A glazed paper stock provides a better and more durable cover. For hard- or soft-cover texts being considered for use in very humid areas, additional attention needs to be given to the quality of paper. Some paper stock warps and discolors badly in extreme humidity. For either type of text, the smaller octavo size tends to be more durable than the larger sizes.

17. *Quality of editing and publishing.* It may require a rather careful examination to discover the quality of editing. Quality, here, is revealed through such things as effective choices of type face, absence of typographical errors, and removal of the author's oversights. Effective use of light and dark type and contrasting type sizes and styles can add considerably to the ease with which the student discerns the organization within the book. Misprints which are obvious to a native speaker may be confusing or misleading to a student. And even the best authors may make an occasional slip in

small details. For example, if in Lesson 3 the seven days of the week are taught and discussed, while the author has just taught the numbers one through five in Lesson 2, a careful editor would have suggested the necessary revision.

The quality of publishing, quite apart from matters of durability, can be seen in attention to details of interest and attractiveness in the book. The cost of color is no longer as prohibitive as it once was. Its effective use in illustrations and diagrams can produce a lively and attractive volume. The inclusion of maps, even on the end sheets, may make the book more interesting. Such maps should be simple enough to be read easily and uncluttered by trivial details. Occasionally, student aids such as phonetic display of the sound system are printed inside the cover. A colorful, well-designed cover reflects the skill and interest of the publisher in packaging his product.

18. *Price and value.* Price is often an extremely significant criterion. Frequently, choices must be made within certain price limits. Sometimes, unfortunately, such limits may remove from consideration one or more of the best available texts. If so, then the matter of price and value comes down to the question: Is this the best for the price within our limits? Making such a decision involves consideration of the evaluator's cumulative judgments about the suitability of the text for its intended use, its promise of durability, and its price. Then, a judgment should be made about the relationship of its value to its price; in other words, "How much of what we hoped for are we getting for our money?" Comparison of several books in this way should help to reveal the best bargain among them. Perhaps, if one text demonstrably offers a much greater value, a prior decision about price limits may be amended to permit its purchase.

RATING SCHEME AND DISPLAY FORM

The rating scheme presented here is probably best discussed in terms of its functions on the display form. Two separate scales serve as the basis for the rating scheme. The first of these, the value scale (VS), appears in the first column on the rating form. This scale consists of the numbers 0 through 5. By means of this scale a relative weight is assigned to each criterion; the most important criteria receiving a score of 5, and any totally lacking in importance a score of 0. On the form displayed here, relative weights have been arbitrarily assigned to the criteria to create what is, hopefully, a broadly applicable value scale.

This value scale, however, is highly flexible. And its flexibility influences the entire rating scheme. If an evaluator finds that any of the criterion value scores shown here fail to reflect the importance of those criteria in the teaching situation for which he is considering a book, he is quite free to substitute any other number from 0 through 5 as value scores. The second column on the display form, a blank column, is provided for these reinterpreted value scale scores. If, for example, a book were being evaluated for use by teachers who were native speakers of English, criterion 13 would be rightfully reinterpreted as 0. The only limitation on such reinterpretation is that the value score must always be expressed in the range 0 through 5.

The merit scale (MS), the second of the two scales in the rating scheme, appears on the display form in the column immediately to the right of the criteria. This scale is used to express the evaluator's judgment of the book as measured by each of the criteria. These judgments are expressed numerically in the range 0 through 4. If the book, measured by a specific criterion, appears virtually ideal in respect to that criterion, its merit should be scored as 4. On the other hand, if the book reveals a total lack of merit in some respect, its merit score on that criterion is obviously 0. For convenience, 1 might be considered as weak, 2 as fair, and 3 as very good.

Displaying an evaluation on the form involves the following steps. First, the evaluator decides to use the value scale presented in column 1 or to arrive at a suitable reinterpretation, which is then entered in the second, blank, column under VS. Second, the book is assessed in terms of each criterion and a merit score for each criterion is entered in the MS column.

COMPARATIVE DISPLAY FORM

Title_____   Author _____

VS		CRITERIA	MS	VMP
		PRONUNCIATION CRITERIA		
5		1. Completeness of presentation	1.5	7.5
5		2. Appropriateness of presentation	1.5	7.5
4		3. Adequacy of practice	2	8
		GRAMMAR CRITERIA		
5		4. Adequacy of pattern inventory	3	15
4		5. Appropriate sequencing	2.5	10
4		6. Adequacy of drill model & pattern display	3	12
4		7. Adequacy of practice	3	12
		CONTENT CRITERIA		
4		8. Functional load	3	12
4		9. Rate & manner of entry & re-entry	25	10
4		10. Appropriateness of contexts & situations	1	8
		GENERAL CRITERIA		
5		11. Authenticity of language	2	10
3		12. Availability of supplementary materials	4	12
3		13. Adequate guidance for non-native teachers	1	3
3		14. Competence of the author	2	6
2		15. Appropriate level for integration	3	6
1		16. Durability	2.5	2.5
1		17. Quality of editing & publishing	3.5	3.5
1		18. Price & value	3.5	3.5

VS—Value Scale   Range 0-5
MS—Merit Scale   Range 0-4
VMP—Value-Merit Product

Evaluated by _____

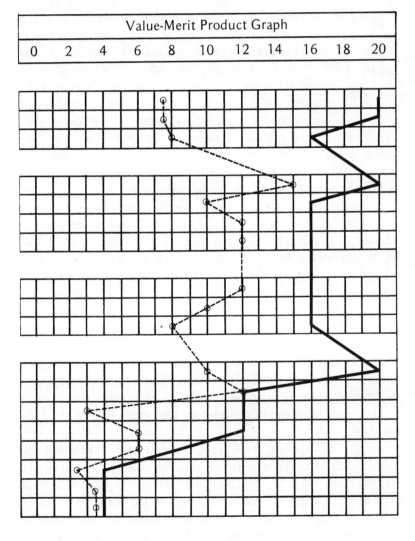

Value-Merit Product Graph

| 0 | 2 | 4 | 6 | 8 | 10 | 12 | 14 | 16 | 18 | 20 |

——— Ideal Profile (Value Score times perfect Merit Score of 4)

----- Profile of Text Analyzed (Value Score times Merit Score)

Third, for each criterion, the product of the value score times the merit score is entered in the VMP column. In this score, the weight of the importance of the criterion and of the merit of the book are combined. Fourth, to produce a graphic display of the evaluation, the number in the VMP column after each criterion is represented on the graph *by placing a dot at the point on the line which corresponds to the numerical value of the VMP score.* For example, for a criterion whose VS score is 4 and whose MS score is 3, the VMP score is 12. Thus, a dot should appear on the graph to the right of the VMP score on vertical line number 12. Dots representing odd-numbered VMP scores are placed midway between the even-numbered vertical lines. Fifth, a line is drawn connecting the dots, producing a line graph of the total evaluation. On the chart, this is the lighter line connecting the clearly defined dots.

In order to show graphically how near or how far the book is from the ideal on any criterion, or in total, a line graph is drawn displaying the hypothetical ideal version of the book. This is achieved by multiplying the value scale score for each criterion by a perfect merit score of 4. A dot is entered on the graph at the point which corresponds to the resulting VMP score. On the form displayed here, these dots (which are *not* shown) are connected by a *heavy line* to make them readily distinguishable from the evaluation graph.

An evaluator can display his opinions of several books on a single form using a different-colored graph line for each book. In this way, he can compare the profiles of the various books and see all of them in contrast to the heavy line of the ideal profile.

If the evaluations of several people must be compared and contrasted in order to reach a consensus, several opinions of a single book may be displayed on one form. Also, if a mean evaluation is desired, it can be added on the form. In this way, a committee can compare individual opinions, the mean of these opinions, and ideal profile. Where a larger group may be involved, use of an overhead projector facilitates the viewing of cumulative display forms. If display forms are to be used frequently, printing them on plastic sheets makes their comparison easier.

Regardless of how the evaluative data are viewed, their presentation by means of the rating scheme and display form suggested here enables an individual or group to focus attention on areas of significant difference of opinion. Not only are the differences among various books specifically and qualitatively portrayed but, in the case of committee evaluations, instances of markedly variant evaluation can be noted and defended or revised.

APPENDIX 4

GRAPH FOR ESTIMATING READABILITY —EXTENDED
Edward Fry

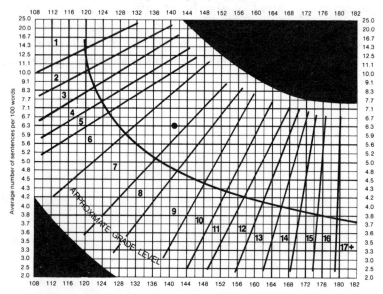

Average number of syllables per 100 words

DIRECTIONS: Randomly select 3 one hundred word passages from a book or an article. Plot average number of syllables and average number of sentences per 100 words on graph to determine the grade level of the material. Choose more passages per book if great variability is observed and conclude that the book has uneven readability. Few books will fall in gray area but when they do grade level scores are invalid.

Count proper nouns, numerals and initializations as words. Count a syllable for each symbol. For example, "1945" is 1 word and 4 syllables and "IRA" is 1 word and 3 syllables.

EXAMPLE:

	SYLLABLES	SENTENCES
1st Hundred Words	124	6.6
2nd Hundred Words	141	5.5
3rd Hundred Words	158	6.8
AVERAGE	141	6.3

READABILITY 7th GRADE (see dot plotted on graph)

EXPANDED DIRECTIONS FOR WORKING READABILITY GRAPH

1. Randomly select three (3) sample passages and count out exactly 100 words beginning with the beginning of a sentence. Do count proper nouns, initializations, and numerals.
2. Count the number of sentences in the hundred words estimating length of the fraction of the last sentence to the nearest 1/10th.
3. Count the total number of syllables in the 100-word passage. If you don't have a hand counter available, an easy way is to simply put a mark above every syllable over one in each word, then when you get to the end of the passage, count the number of marks and add 100. Small calculators can also be used as counters by pushing numeral "1," then push the "+" sign for each word or syllable when counting.
4. Enter graph with *average* sentence length and *average* number of syllables; plot dot where the two lines intersect. Area where dot is plotted will give you the approximate grade level.
5. If a great deal of variability is found in syllable count or sentence count, putting more samples into the average is desirable.
6. A word is defined as a group of symbols with a space on either side; thus, "Joe," "IRA," "1945," and "&" are each one word.
7. A syllable is defined as a phonetic syllable. Generally, there are as many syllables as vowel sounds. For example, "stopped" is one syllable and "wanted" is two syllables. When counting syllables for numerals and initializations, count one syllable for each symbol. For example, "1945" is 4 syllables and "IRA" is 3 syllables, and "&" is 1 syllable.

Note: This "extended graph" does not outmode or render the earlier (1968) version inoperative or inaccurate; it is an extension.

BIBLIOGRAPHY

Achebe, Chinua. 1967. *A Man of the People.* Garden City, New York: Doubleday & Company, Anchor Books.

"Aecerbot" in Albert C. Baugh, ed. *A Literary History of England.* New York: Appleton-Century-Crofts, Inc., 1948, p. 41.

Aesop. "The Crow and the Pitcher," *Aesop's Fables.* Kingsport, Tennessee: Grosset & Dunlap, 1947, p. 58.

Allen, W. Stannard. 1959. *Living English Structure.* 4th ed. London: Longmans.

Anderson, Sherwood. 1923. "I'm a Fool." In *Horses & Men: Tales Long & Short From our American Life.* New York: B.W. Huebsch.

Arbuthnot, May Hill. 1957. *Children and Books.* Rev. ed. Chicago: Scott Foresman.

Bailey, Richard W., and Jay L. Robinson, eds. 1973. *Varieties of Present-day English.* New York: The Macmillan Company.

Bodman, Jean, and Michael Lanzano. 1975. *No Hot Water Tonight.* New York: Collier Macmillan International, Inc.

Bolinger, Dwight. 1975. *Aspects of Language.* 2d. ed. New York: Harcourt Brace Jovanovich.

———. 1968. "The Theorist and the Language Teacher," *Foreign Language Annals.* 2:1 (October):30-41. Reprinted in Harold B. Allen and Russell N. Campbell. *Teaching English as a Second Language: A book of Readings.* 2d ed. New York: McGraw-Hill, 1972, pp. 20-36.

Bowen, J. Donald. 1966. "A Multiple-Register Approach to Teaching English. *Estudos Lingüísticos, Revista Brasileira de Lingüística* Teórica e Aplicada:35-44. Published by the Centro de Lingüística Aplicada do Instituto de Idiomas Yazagi, Sao Paulo, Brazil. Reprinted in Kenneth Croft, ed. *Readings on English as a Second Language.* Cambridge, Mass.: Winthrop Publishers, 1972, pp. 409-421.

———. 1975. *Patterns of English Pronunciation.* Rowley, Mass.: Newbury House Publishers.

Carroll, George R. 1967. "The Battle for Better Reading." *English Language Teaching* 22:1 (October):34-40.

Celce-Murcia, Marianne. 1974. "Teaching the English Modal Auxiliaries." Lecture at University of California, Los Angeles, July 17, 1974.

Chaucer, Geoffrey. "General Prologue," *The Canterbury Tales.* In E.T. Donaldson, ed. *Chaucer's Poetry: An Anthology for the Modern Reader.* 2d ed. New York: Ronald Press, 1975, pp. 24-25.

Dale, Edgar, and Jeanne S. Chall. 1948. "A Formula for Predicting Readability: Instructions." *Editorial Research Bulletin* 27 (January 21), 37-54.

Dale, Edgar, and Joseph O'Rourke. 1976. *The Living Word Vocabulary.* Chicago: Field Enterprises Educational Corp.

Davis, Frederick B. 1967. *Philippine Language-Teaching Experiments.* PCLS Monograph No. 5. Quezon City, Philippines: Alemar-Phoenix Publishing House.

Dintenfass, Phyllis, and Mark Dintenfass. 1967. *How To Adapt and Use Reading Materials.* Nairobi: Oxford University Press.

Donne, John. "Meditation." In Helen Gardner and Timothy Healy, eds. *John Donne: Selected Prose.* London: Oxford University Press, 1967, pp. 100-101.

Eckersley, C.E., and J.M. Eckersley. 1960. *A Comprehensive English Grammar for Foreign Students.* London: Longmans.

Ellison, Ralph. 1975. "Did You Ever Dream Lucky?" In Lillian Faderman and Barbara Bradshaw, eds. *Speaking for Ourselves.* Glenview, Illinois: Scott Foresman.

Evans, Bergen, and Cornelia Evans. 1957. *A Dictionary of Contemporary American Usage.* New York: Random House.

Finocchiaro, Mary. 1969. *Teaching English as a Second Language.* Revised and enlarged. New York: Harper & Row.

Fisher, John L. 1958. "Social Influences on the Choice of a Linguistic Variant." *Word* 14:1 (April):47-56. Reprinted in Dell Hymes, ed. *Language in Culture and Society.* New York: Harper & Row, 1964, pp. 483-488.

Frank, Marcella. 1972. *Modern English: A Practical Reference Guide.* Englewood Cliffs, New Jersey: Prentice-Hall.

Gleason, H.A. 1965. "Language Variation." In *Linguistics and English Grammar.* New York: Holt, Rinehart & Winston.

Goldschmidt, Walter. n.d. "A Word in Your Ear: A Study in Language." Ways of Mankind Series. A tape recording of a radio broadcast. Los Angeles: UCLA, ca. 1958.

Hagerty, Timothy W., and J. Donald Bowen. 1973. "A Contrastive Analysis of a Lexical Split: Spanish hacer to English do/make/etc." In Rose Nash, ed. *Readings in Spanish-English Contrastive Linguistics.* Hato Rey, Puerto Rico: Inter-American University Press, pp. 1-71.

Hall, Eugene J. 1974. *Grammar for Use.* Vols. 1 & 2. Silver Spring, Maryland: Institute of Modern Languages.

Halliday, M.A.K., Angus McIntosh, and Peter Strevens. 1964. *The Linguistic Sciences and Language Teaching.* London: Longmans.

Harris, Joel Chandler. 1955. "Brer Rabbit and the Little Girl." In *The Complete Tales of Uncle Remus.* Boston: Houghton Mifflin, p. 126.

Hayes, Eloise, and Richard Via. 1973. "A Lesson in Creative Dramatics." *English Teaching Forum,* 11:3 (June-August):18-21.

Hemingway, Ernest. 1927. "The Killers." In *Men without Women.* New York: Charles Scribner's Sons, pp. 78-96.

Hines, Mary Elizabeth. 1973. *Skits in English as a Second Language.* New York: Regents.

Hook, J.N. 1965. *The Teaching of High School English.* 3d ed. New York: Ronald Press. 4th ed. 1972.

Hornby, A.S. 1974. *Oxford Advanced Learner's Dictionary of Current English.* New ed. London: Oxford University Press.

Joos, Martin, ed. 1962. *The Five Clocks.* Research Center in Anthropology, Folklore & Linguistics Publication 22. Bloomington: Indiana University.

Juda, L. (narrator). 1963. "The Turban." In *The Wise Old Man: Turkish Tales of Nasreddin Hodja.* Edinburgh: Thomas Nelson and Sons Ltd., pp. 5-7.

Kaufman, Bel. 1964. *Up the Down Staircase.* New York: Avon Books.

Kettering, Judith Carl. 1975. *Developing Communicative Competence: Interaction Activities in English as a Second Language.* Pittsburgh: University of Pittsburgh Press.

Labov, William. 1966. *The Social Stratification of English in New York City.* Washington, D.C.: Center for Applied Linguistics.

Lloyd, Donald J., and Harry R. Warfel. 1956. "Thirty Years to a More Powerful Vocabulary." In *American English in Its Cultural Setting.* New York: Alfred A. Knopf, pp. 432-445. Reprinted in Graham Wilson, ed. *A Linguistic Reader.* New York: Harper & Row, Publishers, pp. 205-215.

Marckwardt, Albert H., and Randolph Quirk. 1964. *A Common Language: British and American English.* London: Cox and Wymar Ltd.

McConochie, Jean A. 1975. *Twentieth Century American Short Stories.* New York: Collier Macmillan International.

McIntosh, Lois. 1974. "Calm or Chaos in the Classroom." *Workpapers in Teaching English as a Second Language* 8 (June):83-86.

Mittins, W.H., Mary Salu, Mary Edminson, and Sheila Coyne. 1970. *Attitudes to English Usage.* London: Oxford University Press.

Morely, Joan. 1972. *Improving Aural Comprehension.* "Teacher's Book of Readings" and "Student's Workbook." Ann Arbor: The University of Michigan Press.

Oxford University Press. 1973. *The Bellcrest Story.* London: Oxford University Press.

Paulston, Christina Bratt. 1970. "Structural Pattern Drills: A Classification." *Foreign Language Annals* 4:2 (December):187-193. Reprinted in Harold B. Allen and Russell N. Campbell. *Teaching English as a Second Language: A Book of Readings.* 2d ed. New York: McGraw-Hill, 1972, pp. 129-138.

Paulston, Christina Bratt, and Mary Newton Bruder. 1976. *Teaching English as a Second Language: Techniques and Procedures.* Cambridge, Mass.: Winthrop Publishers.

Pooley, Robert C. 1974. *The Teaching of English Usage.* Urbana, Illinois: National Council of Teachers of English.

Prator, Clifford H. 1965. "Development of a Manipulation-Communication Scale." *NAFSA Studies and Papers,* English Language Series, No. 10 (March):385-391. Reprinted in Harold B. Allen and Russell N. Campbell. *Teaching English as a Second Language: A Book of Readings.* 2d ed. New York: McGraw-Hill, 1972, pp. 139-145.

Quirk, Randolph, and Sidney Greenbaum. 1973. *A Concise Grammar of Contemporary English.* New York: Harcourt Brace Jovanovich.

Quirk, Randolph, Sidney Greenbaum, Geoffrey Leech, and Jan Svartvik. 1972. *A Grammar of Contemporary English.* New York: Seminary Press Inc.

Reed, Ishmael. 1975. "Necromancers from Now." In Lillian Faderman and Barbara Bradshaw, eds. *Speaking for Ourselves.* Glenview, Illinois: Scott Foresman.

Rist, Ray C. 1970. "Student Social Class and Teacher Expectations: The Self-Fulfilling Prophecy in Ghetto Education." *Harvard Educational Review* 40:3 (August):411-451.

Rivers, Wilga M. 1972. "Talking Off the Tops of Their Heads." *TESOL Quarterly.* 6:1 (March):71-81.

Rosenthal, Robert, and Lenore J. Jacobsen. 1968. "Teacher Expectations for the Disadvantaged." *Scientific American* 218:7 (April):19-23.

Rutherford, William E. 1968. *Modern English: A Textbook for Foreign Students.* New York: Harcourt, Brace & World.

———. 1975. *Modern English.* 2d ed. 2 vol. New York: Harcourt Brace Jovanovich. Vol. 1, 1975; Vol. 2, 1977.

Salinger, J.D. 1945. *The Catcher in the Rye.* New York: The New American Library.

Short, J.A. 1974. "Effects of Medium of Communication on Experimental Negotiation." *Human Relations* 27:3 (March):225-234.

Shuy, Roger W. 1973. "Language and Success: Who are the Judges?" In Richard W. Bailey and Jay L. Robinson, eds. *Varieties of Present-day English.* New York: Macmillan, 1973.

Slager, William R. 1972. *English for Today, Book One: At Home and at School.* 2d ed. New York: National Council of Teachers of English.

Stevick, Earl W. 1959. " 'Technemes' and the Rhythm of Class Activity." *Language Learning* 9:3-4:45-51. Reprinted in Harold B. Allen and Russell N. Campbell. *Teaching English as a Second Language: A Book of Readings.* 2d ed. New York: McGraw-Hill, 1972, pp. 88-94.

———. 1971. *Adapting and Writing Language Lessons.* Washington, D.C.: Foreign Service Institute.

Thomas, Dylan. 1954. "Holiday Memory." In *Quite Early One Morning.* London: J.M. Dent & Sons Ltd., 1954.

Thorndike, E.L., and Irving Lorge. 1944. *The Teacher's Word Book of 30,000 Words.* New York: Columbia University, Teacher's College.

Twaddell, Freeman. 1973. "Vocabulary Expansion in the ESOL Classroom." *TESOL Quarterly* 7:1 (March):61-78.

Velder, Milton, and Edwin Cohen. 1973. *Open-ended Stories.* New York: Globe Book Co.

Velder, Milton, Edwin Cohen, and Elaine Fisher Mazzarelli. 1976. *Open-ended Plays.* New York: Globe Book Co.

Via, Richard A. 1975a. "English Through Drama." *English Teaching Forum* 13:1-2:158-162.

———. 1975b. "Never on Wednesday." *English Teaching Forum* 13:1-2:163-166.

West, Michael. 1953. *A General Service List of English Words.* Revised and enlarged. London: Longmans.

Wolff, Leslie, and Geoffrey Spencer. 1966. *The Modern Children's Library of Knowledge. Book One: The World of Nature.* London: The Grolier Society, Ltd., pp. 55-58.

Wonderly, William L. 1968. *Bible Translations for Popular Use.* Vol. 7. Ann Arbor: Cushing-Malloy, for the American Bible Society.

INDEX